Heritage Quest

Uncovering Your Roots

Heritage Quest

Uncovering Your Roots

By

Jami Lynn Sands

Images by Microsoft
Cover design by Carey Mozena

Sands of Time Publishing
Made in USA

ACKNOWLEDGEMENTS

To my family
for their never ending faith in me
and unwavering support.

To Greg Parks, Editor
for publishing my column
as a community service.

To friend, Randy Neff,
for his willingness to share his knowledge with myself
and the readers, as well as his experience
and dedication to preserving our history.

To colleagues and friends,
Beverly Kerr, Carey Mozena and Rick Booth
for their generous time, and technical skills.
You truly are "earth angels".

To the many library employees and
the Genealogy Society volunteers
who have been so helpful over the years
in assisting me with my research.

To you, the readers of my books and columns
for your kind words and encouragement.

PROLOGUE

And the point is...

As we reach 50 plus, if we haven't already done so, we examine our life and wonder if we have made a difference, and if our descendants will know whom we really were.

It all began as an idea to make a "heritage" scrapbook for each of my adult children and soon turned into a quest to locate and document our roots. When I realized I had very little data on our lineage to add to it, I knew I had to do something to make it meaningful. But what were the facts and who was alive that would have known them? Sadly, there are not many depending on how far back you wish to go.

In researching, I realized that unless you were someone famous, seldom is anything written about you to give any insight into the person you were or what you were about. Imagine how wonderful it would be if every person had left a bit of a legacy recorded for the generations to come.

This book is about learning to help each other do so. Its purpose is to offer ideas and tips to assist you in your quest to uncover the past. It will also offer you creative ways to preserve the information you uncover.

*****

The why of it...

Genealogy (literally meaning the study of one's genes) is meant to be a recorded history of a person's lineage. Those who do not understand its purpose may see it as unimportant or as a way of living in the past. Nothing could be farther from the truth. When working to preserve your heritage, it is important to see what you can uncover about your family tree. What you may find will both surprise and delight you. Generations to come will be grateful that you cared enough to preserve it for them.

Whenever possible, it is important to know something about our history from a medical standpoint. In addition, it can help us to understand genetically how we have come to be the person we are. When we don't understand the why of it or the source of certain traits, it can be very difficult to move forward. It is also helpful to know if any of our ancestors faced similar issues and how they handled them.

Knowing who we are and where we came from is only the first benefit of genealogy research. More importantly, as you research, you will become aware of relatives, no matter how distant, that you didn't even know you had. New relationships with family are built through research, contact and networking. You never know who will come into your life; some maybe for just a little while, others will stay a lifetime. New friends will be made with others who have a passion for research and networking. These friendships too, can last a lifetime.

Yes, life gets in the way and work responsibilities take over our lives. A lot of the household chores simply have to be done eventually. All too often relationships are put on the

*back burner, because everyone is busy and time goes by.
Soon the time comes when it's too late to ask the questions
we wanted to ask or visit the people we wanted to know
better. The longer we wait, the more faded their memories
become, and the more difficult it is to get accurate
information. It really is true that time waits for no one.*

*Grandma knew what she was talking about when she
said, "It'll still be there when you're dead and gone". She
couldn't have put it any plainer that what we think matters,
matters little in the overall scheme of things. It is the quality
time we spend with others that lasts and teaches us life's
lessons.*

*Therefore, I cannot stress enough the importance of not
putting off getting to know extended family. Interview them
now for their point of view on the family heritage. Many of
them have forgotten more than we ever knew about our own
lineage. With a little memory jogging and the right
questions, it is amazing what comes back to them. Each
person you interview will offer a different perspective.*

*Yes, it can be time consuming, but it needs to be done
now before it's too late, and while there are still living
contacts, that you can build a relationship with. Whether you
are a senior wanting to live life to the fullest, someone
pursuing a career, a busy mom, or somewhere in between,
this book is dedicated to helping you make the most of the
resources and time you have. The biggest cost IS your time
and I promise, you will be so glad you invested in it. It is
part of the legacy we leave for future generations.*

*I am often asked, what is the point if I have no children
to leave it to? If you have no heirs, give it to other family*

members. Otherwise, donating it to the library or local genealogy society is the ideal place for such a journal to leave your mark on history. And so the quest begins... revisiting the past through genealogy...enjoy your journey.

*****

Although every effort has been made to maintain the accuracy and verify the information contained, I acknowledge that the words are my own and therefore may contain errors. All websites suggested were active at this writing.

You will also find a bit of what may seem like repetition in some chapters. In these cases, the point is so important that it bears repeating. It is my utmost desire and intention that this information be beneficial to you.

*****

Contents

Chapter One

GETTING STARTED

Setting Goals & Making it Happen

Once you realize that the time period to acquire good information is as limited as life itself, set some timeline goals and do your best to adhere to them. Nothing is more motivating, especially when you see how one clue leads you to several more. However, your first goal is to get organized by deciding on how you want to store and use your acquired information. Then you can begin with information you already have available to you as suggested in further chapters.

*****

Getting Organized

As you might guess, just like with everything else, good organization is essential to making the most of our genealogy research materials and our precious time. One of the most important things we can do for ourselves is to bring order into our lives, and not only with our genealogy research materials, but also with our personal lives. Dumping the clutter helps rid us of negative energy. You will feel so much more like pursuing other interests with freed up time and space to work in. The more organized we are, the easier and smoother it flows. If you have computer access, there are many good software programs available to help you keep it organized. Costs will vary and you may even find some basic ones free online. You can also organize it yourself with an office/word program, by creating various files and folders. (See chapter on "Using the computer"). For those who do not want to invest in learning computer software or do not have a computer or basic computer skills necessary to do so, there are other tried and true methods of staying organized, as evidenced below. However, for the countless bits of information such as photocopies, notes, photos, clippings, etc. you will discover while you are researching, a hands-on system is still necessary for organization.

You will want to use whatever method is easiest for you and best motivates you. Also consider what will best keep your information properly organized.

There are a couple of tried and true methods to choose from.

The following are some resources you will need, as well as a couple of suggested methods (A or B) to choose from; or create your own system with a combination that works for you.

(A) Start with **expandable file folders** and either a plastic crate, a plastic storage bin with a lid, a file cabinet or anything else you can keep your file folders in along with a pad of **sticky notes**. Make a list of all surnames on both sides of the family. Write a surname on each tab or sticky note and attach to a folder. As you accumulate data, such as copies of census, birth, death, marriage certificates, etc. you can file them appropriately. You can then take the file folder you are working on with you in your research.

(B) Use a **soft cover notebook or binder**. A report-cover (lighter weight for portability) works well temporarily, and don't forget a **3-ring punch**, to punch holes in your accumulated documents. However, it is a good idea to choose one that already has pockets or add the cellophane pocket pages to it for tucking in documents that you don't want to punch holes in, such as photos, birth/marriage/death certificates, etc. You can use tabbed dividers for each surname or simply make your own dividers with cardstock. Again, it's portable enough that you can take it with you in your research. This way you can avoid making duplicates of info you may already have.

You will also need a **spiral bound notebook** for taking good notes. Choose one with pre-punched holes. It will make it easier for organizing in case you decide to use the data in a binder at a later date. Or you can carry loose-leaf pages with you to interview if you are planning on using a binder to insert them into.

If you haven't already gotten a **"timeline" diary** started (please refer to the chapter on "Journaling"), start one by recording significant moments and events as the year progresses, while you also work on it retrospectively. Eventually, you will be referring to it often to answer questions as well as help with the timelines in your genealogy research. Present and old calendars you have written on can be a great source for jogging the memory.

Another important organizational tool you will definitely want, are **genealogy forms**. They may include generational charts, family group, and individual charts (for each person). While there are a wide variety of formats available to choose from, choose one that is easiest for you to work with. These can usually be obtained at local genealogy societies, some libraries and/or many online sites free for the downloading or for a nominal fee. Filling these out will help you to keep the generations straight in your mind and make it less confusing. (If you don't yet have the forms, you can temporarily write it out on paper).

Fill in What You Already Know

Once you have your chosen formats of genealogy forms in hand, start by filling in as much as you know now. Of course, it is usually easiest and best to start with your parents, since you no doubt have more information available to you about them. Then you will work backwards through the generations. Working on more than one side of the family at a time can be confusing, which makes organization all the more important.

Start with a generational chart. This will profile your direct lineage. You will also want to use a separate family group chart on each family to include siblings. Keep these forms filed in the front of your bin or notebook for quick and easy reference. Next, use a form pertinent to an individual's chart. A word about filling in your forms; always use only pencil for ease of changing or adding data as it becomes available. No matter how nice your handwriting may be, it is always best to print out your information on your forms in both upper and lower case lettering, so that it lessens the chance of someone misinterpreting the facts. There may be a lot of blanks on your forms in the beginning, but don't let that discourage you. As you look at the blanks you need to fill in, consider where the most likely place would be to find the answers. You are about to embark on a great adventure. It really is a lot like being a detective.

Begin With the Clues You Already Have

Here it is best to start by gathering all the data and memorabilia you already have pertaining to your ancestors. You will then enter this information into your charts and forms as factual data. You will want to include as much information as you know regarding their full names, birthdates, place of births, marriage dates and locations, dates of deaths, and place of burial. As you go about uncovering the past, always make every attempt to verify the leads you get, through legal documentation before recording it in your journals or albums. This can be obtained through courthouse records, libraries, and cemetery records. You can also double-check your information through census records. If this is not possible, be sure to make note that the information listed was obtained through interviews. Always be sure to ask permission before identifying your source.

Learn to read the clues. When you get a lead in your research, if at all possible, follow up as soon as possible while you are excited about it. One clue will usually yield many more new clues. Leads for researching can be all around us right in our own homes or in the homes of relatives. Hunt up artifacts that have been saved over the years as important papers, gifts, heirlooms, or "souvenirs". In looking for valuable clues to analyze the lives of our ancestors, assemble the following suggested items:

1. Bibles---It was important in some families to record facts of births and deaths in their Bibles, considered the core of their faith, to pass down to future generations.

2. Memorial cards from funeral homes---These contain dates of birth, death and burial, the presiding minister, where they were interred, the funeral home handling the arrangements and sometimes other details.

3. Newspaper clippings---These often feature subjects you are looking for in their finer moments, reflecting their occupations, their family events, such as weddings and birthdays, local gossip columns, or they may showcase their talents, hobbies or interests. These can give you valuable clues to timeframes and locations.

4. Obituaries---Not only do they list relatives and dates, but usually give a brief synopsis of a person's life. It is best to copy these in order to preserve them, as actual newspapers yellow and deteriorate with age because of acids and lignin in the paper. Keep in mind, however, that you must verify any information within for several reasons. It depends on who the informant was. Some information may have been left out either intentionally or accidentally due to their state of mind at the time. Therefore, obituaries may not necessarily be accurate.

5. Diaries or journals---These often contain their feelings and impressions and are valuable in gaining insight into their daily lives. These are usually the basis for the human-interest stories that help us understand who they were and the choices they made.

6. Report cards---These will usually include the name of school, teachers, the subjects studied, their grades and actual handwritten specimens of the parent signatures. In some cases, there may even be handwritten comments about the student by the teachers.

7. Diplomas and award certificates from schools (and other memorabilia) or jobs---These help you to document the timelines so that you can use as clues to other events relating to the appropriate year.

8. Yearbooks---These give great insight into what their lives were like in their younger years, and usually contain photos you can copy and often include comments from classmates.

9. Autograph books---These may reveal their interests, as well as dates, names and places.

10. Old china and dishes---Examine it for dates and places, especially if it is locally made.

11. Book collections---Be sure to check their private book collections for notes as well as for inscriptions and dates, especially if you know that they were cherished pieces. (People have been known to tuck letters, notes, or other keepsakes inside of their favorite books).

12. Cookbooks---These may not only have inscriptions and dates but may also have additional handwritten notes in them or tucked inside. They are a great source for actual handwriting samples.

13. Old postcards and letters---Be sure that you check postmarks for dates and places. These are usually handwritten and therefore are themselves a treasure, being another excellent sample of the ancestor's handwriting style, unless of course, they are from a business. In this case they will have historical value.

14. Important papers---These may include, but are not limited to deeds, titles, wills, marriage, birth, baptismal, adoption and death certificates. Compare dates. Remember that first, middle and surnames may be spelled multiple ways and that many of our ancestors often went by their middle names.

15. Trunks and chests---Here you will usually find a treasure trove of information from old clothing to their keepsakes and other heirlooms.

16. Handmade items---These include furniture and paintings that may have names and dates on the back or bottom, handmade quilts, needlework or sewing samplers that may also be personalized.

17. Jewelry---This could include lockets, ID bracelets, charm bracelets, or anything with an initial, inscription or insignia that indicates membership in any faith or organizations.

18. Framed pictures---You should check the backs of old framed pictures, be they artwork or family photos. Sometimes valuables were stored **between** the photo and backing. You never know.

19. Photos, photo albums and scrapbooks---Always check the backs of photos for clues. This would be one of the easiest sources of information, if we had all only remembered to mark them as we got them. Unfortunately, we all get busy, thinking we'll do it later and later we often don't get around to it. We all have lots of old photos that are unmarked that we may not have a clue as to who the subjects are. As we research, we may well be able to locate someone who can identify them.

20. Wedding or anniversary memorabilia---such as napkins, matches, etc. They will usually contain names and dates of the event and/or other personalized information.

21. Examine anything you have that you know that ancestors had or loved; you may find a clue.

Time for a Recap

Every once in a while we will need to stop and take stock of the information we have accumulated, before we get too far into it, and it becomes overwhelming. This is true especially if we haven't been diligent about properly filing it. It is very easy to get behind as one lead grows into several and soon we don't remember where we put a particular detail that we found. This means organizing our paper notes, documents, memorabilia, and filing them in some sort of aforementioned system, as well as backing them up on the computer. This can include, but is not limited to, documents, heirlooms, memorabilia, photographs, interview notes, etc.

Only you can decide how detailed you wish it to be. (However, if you limit it, you may be omitting some fascinating facts). Even if we have been at our research for a while, it is always good to review, because new information always comes to light and it is easy to overlook some sources that we may have never even considered.

What we are looking for specifically is anything that will help us to piece together a timeline of our family tree. Sometimes these clues are right in our own homes or the homes of our relatives and we have simply overlooked or forgotten about them.

Other resources you may consider adding for easy reference include:

--Be sure to place your generational genealogy and family charts in the front for quick reference in keeping track of who belongs to whom. Again, always use **pencil** to enter the information for ease of editing.

--A page of surnames and cities/towns (connected to those surnames) to each notebook or folder for easy reference.

--A page of contacts and phone numbers of people who may have information you seek or that you would like to ask or interview. These are not only relatives, but people who knew of that surname, and may have lived in the area, neighborhood, went to school or church with, or was employed by or with them. Oh, and don't forget in-laws and out-laws. You could get some interesting stories.

--It may be necessary to store memorabilia elsewhere, that is too large for the book or folder. Just be sure to include a note of where the keepsakes may be located. Photos could also be included in these files. However, if you have a lot of them, your purposes would be better served to sort them into separate photo-safe file boxes until you can organize them into permanent layouts or albums.

--So that we leave no stone unturned, it's a good idea to also keep a list handy of possible places to look for sources of information, or to verify your facts, such as: libraries, genealogy societies, historical societies, cemeteries, court docket records, census records, on-line genealogy sites and message boards, obituaries, etc.

*****

Chapter Two

USING THE COMPUTER

Keeping Files Organized

Without computer access, you'll find it necessary to rewrite info on each family/person in your research every once in awhile. Otherwise, it will become very confusing and perhaps unreadable as you add info to it. You don't want to find yourself researching information you already have somewhere in your notebooks.

As you can see, there is much to learn and your journals can be as basic or as detailed as you wish them to be. When you have acquired enough information, and before you get to the point that you feel that your notebooks are getting pretty messy, it's time to transfer the accumulated information to the computer. There are a number of genealogical software programs out there if you wish to purchase one and most are user friendly. However, they are not necessary, especially if the budget is tight, as you can organize it yourself with a basic word program.

Time will tell if we have been diligent in preserving the facts, stories and folklore that has been passed down to us by our ancestors. It is easier now, more so than ever, to do just that with the computer. It allows us the ease of moving words and paragraphs around and even offers a spell check. So if you are fortunate to have a computer (you don't even need the Internet just to use a Word program), don't let another day go by without writing something down that you remember about your ancestors. Another wonderful thing about storing it on the computer, you can add, delete, or correct with a Word program, provided you remember to SAVE it.

You can organize your information on your own computer without software, just by creating folders, and typing in or scanning information or documents. Even if you have it in a paper format for portability, backing it up with the computer is excellent and recommended insurance should your notebooks be damaged or lost. You can then burn it to a CD, DVD, or flash/stick memory drive for sharing with other interested family members.

If your notebook is neatly organized, you could scan it directly onto your computer. I am not that neat when I am scribbling down facts. Therefore, it is easier for me to enter it into a Word program as I acquire it. You can do this either in story form or just as a factual accounting. At any point, you can print it out, three-hole punch it, and put it in a report cover or soft binder to take with you wherever you are researching. In this way, you can edit it as new information comes to light. Some of this may seem repetitious but is so important, that it bears repeating.

Here are some suggestions. You might start by creating
a Word document page for **each family member**. Start out
simple with pertinent information like full name, date and
place of birth, parents, siblings and dates if known, education,
known job history, marital history, hobbies, religious
affiliation and anything else that is known or documented
about that person. (If you have enough information that
includes documents, be sure to scan them into your computer;
you could even create a folder for each person instead of just
a document).

Next create folders in your Word program for each
surname within each side of the family. Insert the
appropriate documents into them as you progress. You may
have other online folders pertaining to that particular family
within that folder as well, such as direct lineage generational
charts, family charts, copies of documents like birth,
marriage, death, adoption, immigration certificates, or
newspaper clippings. Consider creating a list of surnames
and/or cities associated with each side of the family for quick
reference when researching. These will also include maiden
names of female descendants as far back as you can reach. It
can also include stepparent surnames to investigate. This is
especially necessary when additional children were born, as
there is also a biological connection. Other documents you
may wish to add to their file folder are accumulated stories
about each person within the family. In addition to profiles
for each individual, you might want to have a document or
file folder for "**couples**" within each family, profiling their
courtship, their marriage, places they are known to have

lived, their descendants, their place of burial and any other pertinent information you have.

Putting folders within folders helps you to keep it all organized. It means less time looking through all of your documents or files and allows you to locate what you are looking for more easily. The faster and easier things flow, the more likely we are to keep up and stay organized. There are also many good software programs you can invest in and keep to organize your information on the computer, saving you countless hours. Some are user friendly with only basic computer skills and some are a little more complicated, but just about all come with detailed instructions. Prices and needed skill levels vary. Accessing, recording and reviewing data should be easy and fun. In selecting a program, look for:

Ease of use---The selected program must be user friendly, meaning easy enough for beginners as well as experienced computer users alike. The program should be well organized and easy to navigate.

Ease of installation & setup—It needs to be simple to install without any errors or confusing steps.

Sets of features—It should include all the features necessary to research and organize your family tree including reports, charts, searching capabilities, web access and insightful ways to store data.

Help/documentation—The chosen software developer should provide ample help in the form of Q &A's, email and optimally phone support, as well as online course/product tutorials. However, actual phone support is becoming increasingly difficult to find. With the tutorials, anyone can learn to use the program and conveniently access customer support if needed.

With advanced genealogy software, you will be able to organize, store and retrieve family history information in formats that suit your research needs.

Internet Resources

In the event that you don't have adequate Internet access on your home computer, you can always use libraries to search genealogy websites. Most libraries will have a subscription to one or more genealogy sites that have "library edition" database information that you can access for free. If there are a limited number of computers available, a time limit could apply. You will be amazed at how fast that time passes, as you will become fascinated with the wealth of information out there.

There are hundreds of research sites online that you can browse at your convenience. Most of the sites will have links to other sites to which you can subscribe for fees ranging from about $20 to over $300. However, if you research all available truly "free" information listed, you can get lots of clues as to where to look for free information or at a nominal cost. If cost is not an issue, then consider subscribing to one of these sites for in-depth research at your leisure. It is absolutely fascinating to browse through census records, ship manifests, etc. There is also much information including forms that may be obtained online for free by just running a **Google** search. Perhaps you never saw a need to learn any history when you were in school because you never thought you would be able to use it. This puts a whole new light on history when it becomes personal. So, plan to become captivated, as you learn about who, where and how your ancestors lived.

First, we will explore alternatives to paying a lot for information. One such site is **RootsWeb.com**. It is a favorite site for many because it is one of the largest and is said to contain over 3 billion names in 300,000 family trees. There are tutorials to guide you through the most productive use of the site. Best of all, it will even allow you to submit any information you already have or update whatever is already listed. This makes it easy to share with others as they share with you. Although it is affiliated with **Ancestry.com**, there is a wealth of information there free for the taking.

There are free charts and forms available to download that will help you stay organized. You can also sign on to message boards and sign up for their newsletters by way of email. It will direct you to those who may have some of the information in the area you need along with their email addresses so that you can correspond with them. Somewhere someone out there knows something you need to know. This site also includes a social security death index, U.S. Town/County Databases, and a **World Connect Family Tree Project**. It is also an affiliate of Ancestry.com, therefore they may currently offer you a free 14-day trial membership to subscribe. At this writing, it is as low as (subject to change) $12.99 a month for an annual U.S. Membership and $24.99 a month for an annual world membership (after the trial period). The annual or quarterly rates reflect a substantial savings from regular monthly rates. To maximize your trial period, choose a two-week time frame when you have a less demanding schedule and can devote the time to having fun researching. When time is a factor in your research, it may be worth the cost to subscribe for a definite time period to give you the opportunity to work on it at home in your leisure.

Another interesting Internet site to do some research with a large amount of free information is **WorldVitalRecords.com.** You'll have access to a wide assortment of records, including the social security death index, immigration records, as well as military data and an assortment of international records including Canada. They are constantly adding new databases, which are free for a time period, so it pays to keep checking back. They do offer unlimited access to some "members-only" information. They currently have an introductory offer of just (subject to change) $49.95 for a 2-year membership, which is considerably less, than most paid membership sites. If you don't find what you are looking for, they also offer a 30-day money back guarantee.

Then there is **GeneaSearch.com.** This one has been compiled largely by visitors to the site, and of course, also has links to other databases. From here you can search these genealogy sites for your ancestors, as well as contribute whatever knowledge you have of your ancestors. Included are free databases on other sites, (great for cross-referencing) and free searches of some of the leading commercial sites and their databases. Check out the genealogy queries, census, birth, marriage, and death records, biographies, and more in these databases. Each database contains different sets of data, so be sure to search all these databases to find your ancestors and surnames. This site is unique in the fact that it offers volunteers to check specific records for you and also gives you the opportunity to list yourself as a volunteer to help others locate specific information you may have access to. It also includes genealogy books available from individuals and societies, a death and marriage index, a military registry and a section to register surnames and view those submitted. Another feature unique to this site is the female ancestor registry. Female ancestors are often hard to find. Because of name changes and lost marriage records, it is sometimes difficult, if not impossible, to find the lineage of our female ancestors. Here you will find a free genealogy database containing female ancestors (submitted by visitors) to help you find your female ancestors and surnames.

There are many other ways to pursue information on the Internet. Simply enter a name on **USApeoplesearch.com** and see what comes up. You can usually pinpoint whether or not it is the person you are looking for, because the places they have lived are listed and sometimes their age, and others in the household. While it won't usually provide much on deceased persons, this list is a good starting point to know where to look for the person's relatives that you may want to interview. For more detailed results, however, you must sign up for a report, which ranges from (subject to change) $14.99 to $39.99. You can also try typing the name into Google. This may or may not produce results. It is especially helpful if they have ever had a blog or website or are mentioned in one. In any case, it will give you more clues as to where to look.

One that you will NOT want to miss, so be prepared to clear your schedule is www.newspaperarchive.com. This one is totally addictive and you can spend hours there without realizing it. There is such a wealth of information that you can access.

These are just some of the most popular resources. You will find many others; and last, but certainly not least, try typing in your ancestor's name on various search engines and see what links come up. You could be pleasantly surprised.

*****

Chapter Three

USEFUL INFORMATION

Ancestry vs. Nationality

Have you ever been asked what nationality you are? While some people refer to the nationality and ancestry question as one and the same, that is not necessarily the case. According to the dictionary, the term "nationality" is defined as:

1. A body of people having the same traditions, language, or ethnic origin and potentially or actually constituting a nation.

2. The state or fact of being related to a particular nation, as by birth or citizenship.

"Ancestry" usually refers to your lineage, which is a line or body of relatives that you are descended from, just as those who come after you are your descendants. With America having become a melting pot of nationalities and ethnic cultures over the years, the true meaning of nationality has somewhat changed. We are now a body of people who have adopted a combination of traditions, customs and multiple languages living within this nation. Therefore, our nationality has become American. Nationality is something you can change by choosing where you wish to reside and by adopting the ways of that country.

One's ancestry, however, cannot be changed no matter where you might choose to live or the customs you choose to practice, because it involves bloodlines and lineage. You cannot change (even if sometimes you might like to) who your ancestors were. Your ancestors are those whom you were descended from. It is your bloodline. It can be, and in fact in a lot of cases we find that it is, a combination of several ethnic lineages. This is what makes the DNA of each of us unique. When you think about it, we all have two sets of grandparents, biologically speaking, and that makes four sets of great grandparents (maybe you were lucky enough to have some adopted ones as well). For example, in my own case, my maternal grandparents migrated here from the Slovakia (then Austria-Hungry) area of Europe around the turn of the last century. One set of paternal great-grandparents migrated here from Germany in the 1800's. Another set from England. Then we find that we have reason to believe that one great grandmother was indeed Native American. You are likely to find that research reveals not only the persons your ancestors were, but also the things that influenced the lives they led. These influences, in turn, have affected us and made us become who we are.

However, time has a way of erasing the facts as well as memories. That is why it is more important than ever to be sure that we do as much as we possibly can now to record and preserve them.

About Surnames

Have you ever wondered where your family surname(s) actually came from? They often stem from a father's name, for example Johnson no doubt meant son of John, etc. Early settlers sometimes took the name of a nearby village, just as towns were often named for a prominent citizen. Occupational names were also used, such as baker, miller, etc. Sometimes surnames were a combination of a family name and places. Native Americans usually took nature and often earth related names. Names were often shortened, especially foreign names for ease of spelling and adapting to their new homeland. It is not unusual to find as many as twelve different spellings for a surname. Names can be traced back to their point of origin and the country your ancestors migrated from. Most first names have a meaning and surnames are often used as first names and middle names; many middle names being the maternal surname.

On the subject of multiple surnames, life spans were not nearly what they are today and it's likely that it may have become necessary for children to be raised by a stepparent, an aunt and uncle, or some other relative or friend. In this case, children might take the surname of that person whether or not they were formally adopted. If the mother was not married and the child had her name instead of the father's, you will then have another avenue to research for your lineage.

When you come to a dead end in your research on a person, consider this possibility. Sometimes even adults would change their names, either because they just didn't like their surname, they wanted to distance themselves from their relatives or maybe just wanted to assume a new identity. Therefore, aliases were not unheard of even back then. Early immigrants to this country had to deal with leaving loved ones behind in hopes of making a new and better life for their immediate families. They faced enormous odds, coming to a foreign land with very little if any resources to start a new life. Sometimes they depended on relatives or friends who had previously made the journey to help them become established. Many of them had to use their bare hands and strong backs to eke out a living in their new land. They also feared persecution and prejudice here in their new country. Early on, some of their fears became reality when they were discriminated against and called names because of their religion or ethnic origins. While prejudice certainly still exists to some extent, it is no longer the social stigma that it once was. Some would purposely take a different name that didn't sound as foreign.

Whether you are just beginning to research or have been working on it for a while, if you haven't already done so, try these tips. In the event that you have already tried them, try again, because you may not have considered all available options. Sometimes things change and new information may have been added/updated. You just never know.

Is your ancestor's name spelled correctly? Can you think of alternate spellings? Some names may have been misspelled at the time they were recorded on documents, especially when they migrated here from another country. Often sloppy data entry work was the norm, and usually originated at the point of departure. Make a list of alternate spellings for both first and especially surname, if you don't find a match for exact spellings. Try searching under their middle names, since it was often customary to be called by a middle name. However, it is not just immigration records that can be erroneously recorded. Consider the possibility of errors in all recorded documents, be they Federal Census, birth, marriage, death records, etc. and check alternate spellings. You might be surprised at what you will find.

Even if you know the person's given or first name, try searching with just the first initial and last name, or perhaps don't use a first name in your search at all. Not only were last names changed by immigrants, a lot of their first names were anglicized from the original spelling. For example, John may have started out as Jan, Mary was probably Maria, George was most likely derived from Juraj, Steven could have been Stefan, Andrew was previously Ondrej, Katarina became Katherine or Kathleen, and so on. Consider these derivations when searching for your ancestors.

Sometimes we can search and search and keep turning up dead ends on certain relatives. I know it can be discouraging, but it is a fun challenge. The joy of making one hit and adding another piece to the puzzle is both exhilarating and addictive. Remember, there are all sorts of possibilities, so be creative and keep at it.

One of my favorite places to search is through the American Family Immigration History Center of the Ellis Island Foundation at **EllisIsland.org**. It does contain ship manifest records. A ship's manifest is a piece of history and history is rarely an easy thing to decipher, but it is well worth doing so. It is like playing the role of a detective, searching for clues to the past. Best of all, the information is FREE, unless you wish to purchase certain memorabilia from them, in which case, any proceeds go to preserve the foundation for generations to come as a part of their history. You can even learn when they most likely migrated here, the names of the ships they sailed on, as well as their ports of call.

I may have mentioned this site before, but you will want to visit this site periodically, as they keep adding features to it. This site is one of the most exciting online tools available for researching your ancestors. Millions of people have found relatives through this site. And if you can spare a few dollars, this is a worthy cause. It is something that MUST be preserved for future generations.

If the subject of surnames interests you and you would like specific information on your surname, family surname history books may be purchased on line from a number of genealogy sites starting at about $40. A lot of surname research has already been done for you. However, it may be in general terms and not be relevant to your specific family.

Locating the Ancestral Village

A fun thing to do is take a trip and go back in time as far as you can reach. You may already have information about relatives that migrated here at or near the turn of the last century, (which is now more than a century ago). This will be your starting point.

Searching solely by surname will probably not result in you're making much progress. As mentioned in the previous section on surnames, this is because it was very common, especially during the influx of European immigrants, for surnames to be either accidentally misspelled in the recording of documents, or the spelling was intentionally changed or even purposely shortened to make adapting to life in their new country easier. It may have also suffered in the translation due to poor penmanship, or perhaps just spelled as it sounded. Likewise, the same surname may appear in a number of distant villages, yet be totally unrelated. So not only is it the key, but it is also vital to your success to locate the ancestral village of those you are seeking information on. Archival records are generally organized this way and can usually be easily accessed, once you know where to look.

While at this writing our country is considered to be only about 236 years old, whereas, the civilization of Europe and most of the rest of the world has a history that goes back not just centuries but millenniums. Therefore, it is likely that your ancestral village was known over the years by multiple names. This can make it very difficult to locate, even on old maps. However, you needn't be discouraged if you only find a county/province name listed in documents. Sometimes immigrants listed their place of origin just by county or province, whatever was correct at that time. This can be extremely helpful in narrowing your search, since there may be several villages in a country with duplicate or similarly spelled names.

Once you have the name of a possible village on a document, it is important to verify it. The best way to verify surnames and village names is to consult with someone who is knowledgeable of that particular region. This is easier than ever thanks to the Internet. Someone familiar with the area will also be able to recognize an old dialect of a language name versus a present day language name. To locate someone with the knowledge needed, consider posting a message on the message boards of genealogy or ancestry sites and you can correspond with them through emails. One such site states that occasionally a village may come up "missing". There can be various reasons, including what we are all too familiar with here, "construction", as well as incorporation of a village into a larger, adjacent town or city, and very commonly the suffix or prefix of a town being either removed or added.

One of the first places to look for information on the origins of your ancestral village are family documents such as passports, correspondence that was sent back home such as old postcards or letters, baptismal/christening certificates and any other documents. Be sure to ask elders for any place names they can recall. Record them phonetically, until you have evidence otherwise.

Next, check out church records in the place of destination. Here you can find records of any immigrant marriages or children born to them. Be sure to ask the minister to look in the actual church records, NOT a church issued certificate, because there could be conflicting information.

Here are some more of the most reliable places to locate clues to an ancestral village:

Check out the **Social Security Administration**'s web site for information on their programs. You may also file a petition with them through the Freedom of Information Act in order to seek information on your ancestor if they were legally employed in the United States in 1936 or after. It should contain their place of birth as well as their mother's and father's names. However, it is best not to rely on the Social Security Death Index, as they are sometimes incomplete.

You might also request information from the **Bureau of Citizenship and Immigration Services** (formerly INS). This could include alien registration forms, first or second filed papers, and naturalization documents. This one may require a wait of several months since the occurrence of 911.

The US Census from 1900, 1910, 1920, may help to locate the person, but usually only gives a country of origin, which is not of much help in locating the village for genealogy purposes. I can personally vouch for the fact that census records can contain conflicting information due to human error or information given by the informant and therefore, may not be reliable. You will want to cross check the information with other documents. However, for some, it may be a clue you didn't have before and certainly worth checking out, if only for other clues they may contain.

US Port of Entry Records/Ship Manifests--Even if you don't know the date of arrival, microfilms of the items are available through the USA National Archives or more conveniently through the Mormon's Family History Center. These should include dates of arrivals for 1902 and after. There is an index of records organized by last name and different ports of call (for example, Port of New York, Boston, etc). As previously mentioned, the Ellis Island Database not only includes the database, but also images of the actual ship's manifests from about 1892 through 1924. Since 80% of all U.S. immigrants between 1892 and 1924 passed through there, it is convenient and easy to access these database records via the web. There are, however, many errors contained in the manifests. Remember to check multiple spellings of the surname.

An indirect method could be called "searching for family and friends". This involves tracing individuals who may have traveled with them, been left behind or met up with them once they arrived in the states. They may have been neighborhood friends, Godparents or social club friends that you can check for. Chances are they settled near someone they knew. Reading through these records may help you locate places and dates, and these are especially useful clues.

Consider checking out old phone books at libraries. Even country phone books for the region are quite helpful with identifying people with similar sounding surnames. It is likely that these names were derived from a longer version of it in years gone by. Most surnames appear to have survived, though the spelling may vary from what you expect. Although descendants may have moved from the ancestral village, it is likely you'll still find some of them nearby. Some European countries do have access to their phone books online. Current phone books may even yield some clues of their descendants.

The Cousin Connection

It can sometimes be very confusing when we try to determine how we might be related to others. Living in small counties where it seems everyone knows just about everyone else, can also mean that a lot of people are related to a lot of others if only by a marriage. In fact, you never know who is related to whom, so it would do to use discretion in conversations.

For the genealogy researcher, it is especially important to understand the pattern because it is so common to find the same names passed down through the generations within the same family. Therefore, we'll need to describe the relationships more accurately. The following definitions should help. (You can also check with www.ancestry.com for further information).

Of course, first cousins are easy to figure out since they are the children of your aunts and uncles and are of your generation. You all have one set of grandparents in common. The best way to try to keep it straight is to remember that it always goes by "generations". Therefore, if you have the same grandparents, they are your first cousins.

Your cousin's children are of the same generation as your children; therefore your cousin's children are second cousins to your children. So second cousins would have the same great grandparents as you, but not the same grandparents.

Your third cousins have the same great-great grandparents, fourth cousins have the same great-great-great grandparents, and so forth.

There is also the "once removed" distinction. When the word "removed" is used it doesn't mean they didn't get along, (although sometimes we might wish we could remove some of our relatives), but is used to describe kinship (how they are related). It indicates that the two people involved are from different generations. You and your first cousins are in the same generation (two generations younger than your grandparents), so the word "removed" is *not* used to describe your relationship. The words "once removed" mean that there is a difference of one generation. For example, your mother's first cousin is your first cousin, but is once removed since she is not of your generation. This is because your mother's first cousin is one generation younger than your grandparents and you are two generations younger than your grandparents. The one-generation difference equals "once removed. "Twice removed" means that there is a two-generation difference. You are two generations younger than a first cousin of your grandmother, so you and your grandmother's first cousin are first cousins, twice removed. However, rather than "removing" anyone from the family, I think we'd do well to find a new term for it. Yes, it can be confusing. Instead of explaining it in detail to those to whom it doesn't matter, it's become acceptable to simply say someone is your second cousin, even if it is technically a generation removed. In any case, generational kinship charts can help you to simplify your search and keep it straight in your mind.

Why should you care who your third, fourth and fifth cousins are? Some people don't care. Besides the obvious objective of locating new relatives, to the serious minded genealogy researcher, it is vital. Among those same cousins, there are probably already some that have tons of information that you are looking for that they would be happy to share with their newfound relatives. The wealth of information we can share and the new friendships we will form are indeed heartwarming.

The History of the Postcard

Be sure to check with your elders. It is a good bet that some of the older generation has saved some old postcards; some may even date back to around the turn of the century (1900). There were different kinds of postcards. Prior to 1898, only the U. S. Post Office could manufacture them. These were generally pretty generic, blank on one side where the sender could write a message and printed postage on the other side with space for a mailing address. In 1898, Congress authorized the use of cards manufactured by others. These cards could not be called "postcards", as this term was restricted to cards printed by the Post Office. Between 1898 and 1901, they were often called "Private Mailing Cards" or "Private Cards". From 1901 to 1907, they were done so that one side was reserved for the address; the other side, undivided could contain any printed or written matter. The picture was often small and many manufacturers tried to leave some white space so the sender could add a written message. Often the sender would write across the picture. And it was in 1901 that manufacturers of private mailing cards were allowed to use the term "postcard". In 1907 until 1915, Congress allowed the back of the card to be divided so that the sender could write a message on the left side of the back and the address to who the postcard was to be sent on the right side. At first, the message area was much smaller than the address area, but eventually the two areas became the same size. Most of these cards were printed in Germany. When World War I broke out, the industry suffered greatly and many of the printing plants were never re-built after the war. After 1915 until about 1930, U. S. Publishers tried to fill the void in the postcard market. To save on the amount of ink per card, publishers left a white border around the edge.

From 1930 to 1945 they became linen. These colorful postcards were mass-produced on a fiberboard that had a linen texture. In 1939, there came another option, chrome, which looks like a full color photograph and is still in use today. There were also real black and white photos where the publisher marked the photo process on the back.

When you locate them, they can yield all kinds of clues. You'll find whom they were sent to, where they were postmarked from, actual handwriting samples, and the message will give you a glimpse into their daily lives. There were also funny postcards back then for those who enjoyed a sense of humor. I have even seen a wooden one from around 1945.

There are also Internet sites on postcards; my favorite being Penny Postcards which is run by the www.USGenWeb.org Archives Website. You will find photos there of the different kinds of postcards. They are not for sale on this site, but available for all to see. Once on the site, go to the state and then the county you want to search in. You can upload these by scanning, but before doing so, please contact the site administrator for more information as to what is accepted at pennypostcards@gmail.com.

*****

Chapter Four

GENERAL RESEARCH

Getting the Facts

While we are in the process of acquiring information through research and interviews, we will need to accumulate the following factual information or as much of it as we possibly can for each person we are researching. Basic information will first be entered into our generational charts, and then into the proper family and individual charts in the format of your choice, the one that makes the most sense to you. Items you might include:

1. Full name, include any nicknames and/or aliases.
2. Birth date and place.
3. Biological parents, stepparents or legal guardians.
4. Siblings, along with their approx. year of birth in order to document the order of the births.

5. Their education, include where they attended or graduated from. Include approximate years, if known.
6. Their profession or trade, including where they worked and any other work history you can find; again include years, if possible.
7. Their marriage(s), date, where and to whom; you might also include where they met their spouse, if you know. (Also include dates or any information on any divorces involved).
8. Their children, names and birthdates.
9. Where they lived, property they owned, and for how long, etc.
10. Their activities, organizations they belonged to, hobbies and interests they enjoyed.
11. Their personality; you will have to rely solely on interviews for this one, if you didn't have personal knowledge of them.
12. Who their friends and neighbors were.
13. Their date of death, place, cause of death and burial site.

Always include a note on your sources of information, especially those requiring legal documentation. In this way, you'll know where to return to this source if need be, and at the same time, add credibility to your work. When listing oral information obtained by interviewing others, be sure to note your source and the date. Since this is a memory of, or reflection from said person, it therefore may or may not be able to be documented.

So as you can see, there is much to learn and your journals can be as basic or as detailed as you wish them to be. When you have acquired enough information, or you begin to feel that your notebooks are getting pretty messy, if you have computer access, it's time to transfer the accumulated information to the computer. There are a number of genealogical software programs out there if you wish to purchase one and most are user friendly. However, they are not necessary, especially if the budget is tight, as you can organize it yourself with a basic word program.

Again, please refer to Chapter Two on using the computer, for more detailed information. If your notebook is neatly organized, you could scan it onto your computer. I am not that neat when I am scribbling down facts, so it is easier for me to enter it into a word program as I acquire it. Word programs, of course, allow you ease of adding or changing your entries. It can be either in story form or just as a factual accounting. You will eventually organize your individual pages into folders. Just always be sure you SAVE it. At any point, you can print it out, three-hole punch it, and put it in a report cover or soft binder to take with you as your research for ease of editing.

Entering it into the computer will also serve as a way to keep things straight and provides back up, should your notebook be damaged or lost. Once you have the information on the computer, be sure to periodically burn it to a CD, DVD, or flash drive as a backup.

Without computer access, you'll find it necessary to rewrite info on each family/person in your research every once in awhile to keep it readable as you add info to it or you may find yourself researching information you already have somewhere in your notebooks.

An idea worth mentioning--for your notebooks or documents, use the little colored post-it tabs anywhere there is something you want to come back to, or further attention is required. On the computer, in a word program, simply highlight that specific area or use a different colored font to draw your attention back to it. Again, always include notes on your sources of information, especially those requiring legal documentation. In this way, you'll know where to return to this source if need be and also add credibility to your work.

Local Research

A good place to start is by locating the Genealogy Society, a Historical Society and/or genealogy rooms of libraries in yours or surrounding counties.

I've been asked about the difference between the **Genealogy Society** and the **Historical Society**. Though they both deal with preserving the past, the Historical Society is particularly good at preserving the history of the local area. They are usually chapters of a National Society. While most county genealogy societies do have some local history, its primary goal is to put together a history of its people. It deals with family histories, as well as the vital records pertaining to individual family members.

There are usually friendly, knowledgeable, unpaid volunteers that are happy to help you, that staff most Genealogy Societies. For that reason, it may be necessary to maintain limited hours, whereas, the libraries have employees and can offer extended hours, which is especially helpful.

The genealogy rooms at local libraries also contain some of these records, some of which they have gotten from the society. (Libraries can usually offer longer hours than volunteer services).

You will find some needed information at both locations. However, there may be some information at each of them that the other doesn't have, so you will want to cross check at both if you are serious about tracking down leads. Some of the resources that may be found there that are especially helpful are:

City and county directories--publications that were sponsored by area businesses, usually annually. You will find information on businesses operating in the city/county in that year, some may even date back to the first half of the last century. They may also contain a list of streets and who lived at the addresses on them at that time. You will find an alphabetical list of family surnames, usually giving spouse name and occupations. Some even list children and the year of their birth.

Vital records-- include marriage, death, wills and estate records from 1800's and well into the 1900's.

Cemetery records--you'll be surprised whom you will find. They include pioneer cemeteries of the county.

Obituaries--on file, though incomplete, you will find some that can give you a little more information than you may have had.

Military records—can include rosters of those who served, possibly dating back to the Revolutionary War, Civil War, and World War I, etc.

Individual family histories--donated to the library or genealogy society.

High School yearbooks—a wonderful resource for finding timelines and are usually donated.

Court docket archives—these may include common pleas and criminal records usually prior to 1940.

Various county histories--for both in-state and out of state (including some vital statistics).

Old newspapers--many dating back from the mid-1800s to present on microfilm. All you need is an approximate date to search the papers for what you are looking for. Some of what you might find there are birth, marriage, and death announcements, society news, accident reports, court news, etc. The older newspapers are fascinating and you may find yourself reading them just to see how previous generations lived.

In addition, both the Genealogy Society and the library offer access to online resources, which include the Federal Census records from 1820 to 1930. So, if you don't have Internet access or your computer is down, you can still research and it is free. (Time limits can apply if there is anyone waiting).

By the way, if you are cleaning out and find any old yearbooks, old telephone books, family histories, historical information, or other memorabilia that you no longer want, please consider donating it to either the library or genealogy society so that others may enjoy and use for reference.

Lifestyles of Our Ancestors

It is absolutely fascinating to catch glimpses into the lives of ancestors and get hints of what their everyday life was like. Keep in mind that they were at a different time and place in history. In some ways they had it much harder than we do; in other ways, they lived a simpler life. Therefore, our lives are much more complicated than theirs were. Our ancestors made their decisions based on what information was available to them at the time. Furthermore, we shouldn't judge them too harshly should we discover that we disagree with a decision that they made. They were human, they made mistakes, and they had great joys as well as sorrows. We have many of the same challenges today, but somehow, the world doesn't see it as the same problem that it often was for our ancestors.

Where do we go to find that information? The first and most obvious place is to interview persons still living who knew them. (Check out the chapter on "Networking"). However, there is always the possibility that their memories may not be accurate or that they simply can't remember.

Occasionally, you will find that they just don't want to reveal what they deemed to be a family secret. We need to respect that in their lifetime, they just are not ready to deal with the revelation and/or what they expect the results could be. Of course, anything that you can get is still better than nothing. Next try land records. Not only will this tell you where they lived and what they owned, but could even tell you what they paid for it, who they bought it from or who they sold it to. Locally, these records are public information and housed at the courthouse. You can then trace back to how long a farm or other property has been in a family.

One of the easiest ways is to use birth and marriage records, along with a little math. This could very well yield some best-kept secrets. The old saying that "the more things change, the more they remain the same", is really true. The difference is, even though we may or may not approve, it is now spoken of and accepted as the way things are; whereas in bygone times, much was kept in confidence.

As for court documents, though you might wish that you wouldn't uncover anything there, you could be surprised at what you discover. There may have been civil or criminal charges brought against them. Even though they may have done nothing wrong, others could have accused them, falsely or not, and it may have gone to court. There may also be a contested will that will surface. This will tell you who did and didn't get along and why. Although it is likely that we could uncover things we would not like to find, remember that it is a part of their history. Any mistakes they made could have been due at least in part, to their circumstances at the time. Here are some other sources:

Commerce/shopping records---Most of us have a mental picture of our hardworking ancestors living off the land, as far as raising and preparing their food, making and sewing their own clothes, bedding, and even tools. They usually made their own soap and some of their furniture, as needed. It's a pretty safe bet, that they also traded goods, livestock, and even exchanged services with other family members, friends and neighbors. Before there were many merchants in this new land, the barter system was the usual form of business. It is well documented that early pioneers also traded with the Native Americans. Sometimes this went well and sometimes it didn't. Eventually little trading outposts began to spring up in the late 1800's.

In the new century, these evolved into mercantile and general stores wherever towns came into existence. As self-sufficient and resourceful as our ancestors were, most took advantage of the opportunity to obtain some "store bought" goods whenever possible. That is, if they were lucky enough to have the means to do so. Getting "store bought" was indeed a treat. (Little did we know that someday "homemade" would become the treat).

Sometimes getting 'store bought" may have meant hitching up the buckboard and traipsing over some very rough terrain. This meant that their little shopping excursions occasionally left a trail of clues at one business or another. No, they didn't have debit or credit cards, pin numbers, or even checks to leave a paper trail. Although business was often conducted with their good name and a handshake, most shopkeepers did keep handwritten ledgers or account books of their daily transactions. The usual purchase may have been flour, sugar, fabric, an occasional cup and saucer, a cooking utensil, or just about anything else that they could not make for themselves. However, people did pay a good bit of cash for alcohol. (Some things never change).

Some shopkeepers also made notes on their regular customers as to where they resided, their occupation, family members, buying habits, and even when they died. Transaction details may have included dates, items and prices paid. Thus these ledgers can be a gold mine of clues.

According to online information, these business records are usually considered historical documents. Therefore, you can find them most often in libraries and archives as part of their manuscripts collections. Conduct your search for business ledgers based on location and time. For online catalogs try a variety of terms: ledger, daybook, journal, account book, retail, general store, and sales. For example, a search of the Ohio Historical Society library catalog yielded forty-six hits using the terms "general store daybook". Use the www.worldcat.org. It is said to be the world's largest online library of materials to search for far-flung records. Even though a nineteenth-century proprietor operated his store in Nebraska, you might find his records in a California library.

You can also check for business records in local repositories where your ancestors lived, such as historical societies, museums, as well as the public libraries. Remember not to limit yourself to the local area they lived in. Consider the fact that they did occasionally make an overland trip to a neighboring county, to a large city, state or territory that was several days' travel away. Your search will be worth the clues it yields.

Their finances---In times gone by, most of the wealth our ancestors possessed was in their land. For centuries, real estate and land holdings have been the subject of everything from wars among nations to family squabbles. Unfortunately, that still holds true for many today. Even those who don't have much else, might at least own their home and the land it sits on. Somehow it doesn't seem fair that we were put on this earth with nowhere else to go, but yet we have to pay for the squatter's rights. How else could we determine who gets to live where?

Another source of wealth to many of our ancestors, that they did not even consider, were their possessions. Most of these were simple and minimal to them, since they were needed for their everyday lives. Little did they realize that these heirlooms would be considered antiques to subsequent generations. Eventually, some of these treasures will command a high price. Therefore, leaving them for their descendants could become a legacy in more than one way.

When much of our country was young, farms prospered, and in addition to meeting the family's needs, the farm could also provide them a good source of income raising food and livestock to sell. Their livestock also meant wool, eggs, milk, and meat either for sale or bartering. Luckily, these practices are particularly alive and well today in the Amish community.

In order to learn about our ancestor's real estate and land holdings, it will be necessary to research public records. These are usually located in the county recorders or auditor's office of the county in which they lived. In some cases, records can go back as far as the early 1800's and are available for the general public to review. Most of these older records have since been transferred to the local library, genealogy, or even historical society. The older bank records in particular, are fascinating glimpses into their lives. Take for example, a bank note to a relative to buy a cow. If one party believes that the note was not properly repaid, then it could provide an answer or at least a clue, to the reason for a rift in the family. You never know what may be uncovered in the course of investigating.

In addition, businesses or professionals, who provided services at that time, may also have records that have survived, which may be accessed. These could be early law firms, physicians, funeral directors, hotel ledgers and just about anything else that they could have availed themselves of. Again, you must first check the archives in local libraries or genealogy societies for these records, because these businesses, in all likelihood, no longer exist.

Any of these avenues can be a rich source of additional information when looking for clues to piece together a family history.

*****

Chapter Five

RESEARCHING THROUGH GOVERNMENT AGENCIES

Military Records

Sometimes, everywhere we turn for information on our early ancestor's military service, we reach a dead end. Maybe all you have to go on is the word of living relatives that someone you are researching did serve in the military. It can be very frustrating.

How did your ancestor serve their country? Your goal may be to find records for the Vietnam Conflict, Korean War, World War I and World War II and even as far back as the Civil War or American Revolutionary War. The easiest place to start for a source of information, is to check with living relatives who may have any of the following types of military memorabilia or records. These can include enlistment records, draft registration cards, prisoner of war records, newsreels, military newspapers, military yearbooks, and also burial registries. However, due to the Freedom of

Information Act, it is very difficult to obtain any records from the government, even though you may be a relative, although not next of kin. This is necessary to preserve the privacy of our veterans, but it isn't of much help when you are searching for genealogy leads. There is, however, a government organization, the **National Archives and Records Administration (NARA)**, which may be of help. If you qualify as next of kin, you may write them for the information you need. There is a form online you can download to send in for a copy or for further information. If you are not next of kin, you may also apply, but you are limited in the type of information you can obtain from them. These records are not available online.

However, some of the records that may be of genealogical interest to you that ARE available on the web site are:

--Casualty lists for World War II, the Korean and Vietnam Wars
--Spanish-American War compiled military service records for the "Rough Riders"
--World War II honor list of deceased and missing Army personnel from 1946
--Records of Duty Locations for Naval Intelligence Personnel, 1942-1945
--Prisoner of War lists for World War II, the Korean and Vietnam Wars
--Fugitive Slave Case Papers, 1850-1860
--Criminal Case Files from Fort Smith, Arkansas and much more.

The site, www.archives.gov is very informative and
offers many tips to follow in your research.

US Census

The first U.S. population census was conducted in 1790
under the direction of Thomas Jefferson, who was at that
time, the Secretary of State. Some, especially the newly
formed states, including Ohio (which had been considered
part of the Northwest Territory), did not participate until
about 1820.

Census records will usually yield multiple clues
(depending on the year), and can include who was living in
the household then, what their occupations were at that time,
all of their ages or year of birth, etc. Most census records for
Ohio, as well as most states, are currently available through
1930 for free to the general public at public libraries and
genealogical societies. If you would like a copy, the average
cost is usually about a quarter per sheet.

The US Census from 1900, 1910, 1920, may help to
locate a person, but usually only gives a country of origin,
which is not of much help in locating the ancestral village for
genealogy purposes. As some have found, census records
can contain conflicting information due to either human error
or inaccurate information given by the informant and
therefore, may not be reliable. You will want to crosscheck
the information with other documents. However, for some, it
may be a clue you didn't have before and certainly worth

checking out, if only for the additional clues they may contain.

The older the census documents, the sketchier they generally are for two reasons: the deterioration of the documents themselves, some being nearly unreadable, and the fact that any documentation at that time was minimal at best. Reading census documents may require some simple math to identify the timeframe for the people you are seeking information on. You will likely encounter multiple generations in a family with the same first names. Another oddity, by today's standards, may surface that was not unheard of around the turn of the century. Evidence exists to show that because the infant mortality rate was so high at the time, they would often use the same name again for another sibling. In this way they honored the memory of the child they lost. Many children of the time died before their first birthday.

Census records are only compiled on the general population near the beginning of each decade. Results are not to be made available to the general public for seventy years, which in actuality, is every seventy-two years. They need time to prepare them. This means that the latest, free public access to the records of the 1940 Census, become available after April 1st of 2012. This is a privacy measure. However, with the new trends in longevity, it is highly likely, some will still be alive when they are released.

That, of course, is too long for most of us to wait for genealogy purposes. However, for those who meet the strict requirements and a fee of $65 (at this writing), it is possible to obtain a copy of the unreleased information on a particular individual prior to that. Use this link for further information:

http://www.census.gov/genealogy/www/agesearch.html
There are also several online services that you can
subscribe to for a fee that will give you at-home access to
their records (including census info but these are dated only
up to 1930). This can be a costly way to go, but you have the
convenience of accessing it at home and at your convenience.
However, there is no guarantee that you will learn anything
you didn't already know from public access resources.

Social Security Administration

You can also check out the Social Security Administration's
web site for information on their programs. It is also possible
to file a petition with them through the Freedom of
Information Act, in order to seek information on your
ancestor, if they were legally employed in the United States
in 1936 or after. It should contain their place of birth as well
as their parent's names. However, do not rely solely on the
Social Security Death Index, as they are sometimes
incomplete.

Bureau of Citizenship & Immigration Services

You can request information from the **Bureau of Citizenship
and Immigration Services (formerly INS)**. This could
include alien registration forms, first or second papers, and

naturalization documents. This one may require a wait of several months since the occurrence of 911.

US Port of Entry Records/Ship Manifests

Even if you don't know the date of arrival, microfilms of the items are available through the **USA National Archives** or even through the **Mormon Family History Center**. These should include dates of arrivals for 1902 and after. There is an index of records organized by last name and different ports of call (for example, Port of New York, Boston, etc.). As previously mentioned, the Ellis Island Database not only includes the database, but also images of the actual ship's manifests from about 1892 through 1924. Since 80% of all U.S. immigrants between those dates passed through there, it is convenient and easy to access these database records via the web. There are, however, many errors contained in the manifests. Remember to check multiple spellings of the surname.

Another method could be called "family and friends". This involves tracing individuals who may have traveled with them, been left behind or met up with them in the States. Neighborhood friends, Godparents and social club friends can be checked. It could be very helpful in tracking them, when your ancestors cannot be located through any other method. Reading their records may help you locate places and dates, and these are especially useful clues.

Don't forget to look through present-day phone books. County/province phone books for the region are quite helpful with identifying people with similar sounding surnames. It is likely that these names were derived from a longer version of it in years gone by. Most surnames appear to have survived, but the spelling may vary from what you expect. Although descendants may have moved from the ancestral village, it is likely you'll still find some of them nearby. Best of all, some European countries do have access to their phone books online.

Ellis Island (and the European Influx)

Ellis Island, now a National Park service destination, is a 27.5-acre site located just minutes off the southern tip of Manhattan Island, New York. From 1892 to 1924, more than 22 million immigrants, passengers, and crew came through Ellis Island and the Port of New York. The ship companies that transported these passengers kept detailed passenger lists, called "ship manifests". Ellis Island is likely to connect with more of the American population than any other spot in the country. It has been estimated that nearly half of all Americans today, myself included, can trace their family history to at least one person who passed through the Port of New York at Ellis Island nearly a century ago. According to the website www.ellisisland.org, the Ellis Island Foundation, is a non-profit organization dedicated to the preservation of the island, and the Statue of Liberty. They have established a wall of honor, which is very exciting, and is The American Family Immigration History Center on the island. Best of all, it is also accessible on the web. They have 25 million immigrant arrival records in the Ellis Island archives

available to everyone, currently for free. However, if you
wish, you can purchase your documents from them on
archival paper, which make excellent gifts and proceeds help
them keep the site free. This site also contains a wealth of
additional information.

*****

Chapter Six

RESEARCHING OBITUARIES & CEMETERIES

Using Obituaries for Leads

One would think that obituaries would be a wonderful source for obtaining information on your ancestors and sometimes they are. However, one should always treat them as a source of obtaining additional clues, rather than actual facts and this information must always be verified. Unlike the general reliability of tombstones and grave markers, remember that obituaries are usually submitted by grieving family members, probably on the spur of the moment, and may be incomplete, inaccurate, misleading or worse, all of the above. It is usually not intentional and there are a number of reasons that the information within can be inaccurate.

When there have been multiple marriages, sometimes only the present spouse is listed in the obituary. In this case, children listed may or may not be biological. They could be adopted, stepchildren or a grandchild, niece or nephew, or another relative who was raised by the deceased. This bond may have been a very strong one that both parent and child felt in all the important ways, but it does not help you to identify biological relationships for genealogical and/or lineage purposes. When there is no distinction listed in the obituary, then you must clarify the relationship through birth records.

Inaccuracies can also occur intentionally because of estrangements. This was just as common in our ancestor's time, as it is today. Unfortunately, it does not then give an accurate picture of the deceased's descendants, again, making it difficult to know for sure who or what may have been omitted.

There may also be unintentional errors submitted by the informant, especially when it comes to deceased family members. They may not have known all of the facts, or that there were other siblings, especially if they died in either infancy or childhood.

Yes, obituaries are important to your genealogical research, but always use the information contained with care and as a lead to be checked out. Obituaries are meant to inform the public of someone's passing and give details of the arrangements or memorial service. Treat all other listed information as clues that point to additional information. As you might guess, some clues given besides names of relatives, both living and deceased, are dates of birth, marriage, death, where they received their education, military service, their trade or occupation, affiliations with clubs, organizations, and churches, and any accomplishments they achieved. Luckily, present day obituaries also give the reader a glimpse into the person's life by stating their interests and what was most important to them. A lot of these subjects were omitted from early obituaries forcing the researcher to rely on hearsay and any records they could find.

Where can you check it out and verify information listed? For relatives, both living and deceased, birth, christening and death records are your best source, even though typographical errors are always a possibility. For education, there are school records, report cards, and yearbooks. For military service information, besides checking with living relatives for any documents, try to verify them through government records. Major accomplishments are best documented through newspaper archives, available in most libraries of the county in which they occurred. Bottom line…always be sure that you verify information in obituaries.

About Cemeteries

Some people consider a discussion on the subject of cemeteries to be morbid. Halloween has helped to perpetuate this spooky impression, with stones leaning in all manner of eerie angles. But from a historical point of view, they can be quite fascinating. Furthermore, if you have a strong belief in the hereafter, then you realize it is just another part of living. You eventually come to understand and become comfortable with the circle of life.

From a genealogy standpoint, it can be one of your very best sources of information. Why? Information contained on tombstones is rarely incorrect; and if it were put on wrong, someone will report it and have it corrected. So you can be fairly certain it is accurate.

As cemeteries go, modern trends seem to be running more and more toward the marker only look, without headstones, so that the cemetery can maintain the look of a garden or park. Some of the most beautiful cemeteries in larger cities are definitely "memory gardens" or "memorial parks". Who wouldn't like the idea of their remains going to a park or garden vs. a "cemetery" or the traditional "graveyard"? Thankfully, however, our ancestors had the foresight to place much information on the stones, or there are a lot of facts on tombstones that would have been lost forever.

The next time you have the opportunity to visit a cemetery, take notice of the many different details that can be noted on tombstones. Sometimes maiden names are listed for wives along with their married names. With a little subtraction, you can figure their ages at death and even how they were related to others within the plot. Nowadays, there are often carvings or etchings on the stone that reflect the person's interests and beliefs, giving anyone who views it a glimpse into their life. In present times, it is becoming increasingly common to find an occasional photo of the deceased embedded in the stone. Of course, there will also be flags or markers of military service.

My pick of the most interesting cemeteries are the oldest cemeteries you can find. There you will not only find some long forgotten details, but also see some interesting catch phrases that are more than just amusing. Prewriting one's own epitaph or leaving instructions for doing so was not uncommon back then. The only trouble is, sometimes they become so weathered that parts of the details may be nearly unreadable. They did not have the same materials or treatments for stones in those days that we have available today, and many have no living relatives to see to restoring or repairing them. One of the oldest cemeteries that I, personally, have ever visited was an old Confederate cemetery in the south. It was a truly historical experience.

What if you don't know where an ancestor is buried? Most libraries and genealogy and/or historical societies have records of the cemeteries within a county, as well as private and church cemeteries. You can check these records for your ancestor's names or approximate date of death. The place of interment is often listed in obituaries, giving you another clue as to where to look. For more current death records, you will need to check county or state death records. We are grateful to those who took the time to "read" the stones, record and index them to help make our research easier.

Some Background on Cemeteries

Before you go off to explore the genealogy clues within a cemetery, it may help to know a little about what you are seeing and what to look for. First of all, what is the difference between a graveyard and a cemetery? A graveyard in days gone by was considered to be one that has, or has previously had, a church or chapel on site. A cemetery is one in which it's only purpose is for burial and does not necessarily have a religious affiliation.

What are the differences between a tombstone, a gravestone and a headstone? Sometimes these words are used interchangeably, usually depending on regional practices. However, a tombstone is a grave marker, and is normally flat and lying on the ground. It can be any size, from small to covering the entire length of the grave. A gravestone and a headstone usually refer to a stone set in an upright position that contains information. In some families it is customary to have a separate stone erected with just the family surname on it and then add smaller versions for individual family members.

What is the difference between a mausoleum and a crypt? A mausoleum is an above ground tomb usually designed to inter the remains of multiple persons. The smaller ones are usually family mausoleums, while the larger are more public and may contain the remains of unrelated persons who preferred above ground interment. Mausoleums are usually made of reinforced granite because of its durability to withstand the elements. The word "crypt" was previously used to refer to an underground tomb or burial vault, but in modern times it has also come to refer to any drawer system of entombment. This is particularly relevant depending on the type of mausoleum, whether box or walk-in. Of course, the choice of options is a personal thing for the individual and the family. (For further information on this, check with your local monument company or ask a funeral director for suggestions).

Anyone who has done any research in a cemetery is aware of the genealogical and historical value, but what many may miss is the architectural beauty and artistry involved there. Much of the design used echoes Gothic Cathedral, Classic Revival, Egyptian-influence design and Art Deco.

The following is some helpful information, about what you might see, to assist you in your research.

Tomb/gravestones prior to the 1830's were usually made of sandstone, many from the locality. After that, marble became widely used, but it was necessary to ship it in by rail, since it was not readily available in most locales. Marble was not usually polished until the last century, after the 1900's. Most stones are now made of granite, not only because it is more plentiful, but also much more durable.

The older the stone, the more likely you are to find the age of the deceased in years, months and days, especially for children.

It was also common on older stones for the carver to leave his mark or name near the bottom as a form of advertising. (Tacky though it may have been, ways of advertising in those days were severely limited.)

Another common word often found on old stones was the term "consort of". This term was interchangeable in those times with spouse, usually referring to the wife.

Many older stones also have what might be termed a gabled roof-look or top. Not much is known on this design, but may perhaps have been an attempt to keep the elements from eroding it.

While there are many interpretations of this practice, some commonly held beliefs in Jewish tradition are that several rocks or small stones are placed atop the gravestone symbolic of their loved ones having visited and as a reminder that we are made from the earth.

Plaques used as either grave markers or tribute markers are usually made of bronze, which by composition is usually a combination of copper and tin. For a lasting tribute, no other material is as durable and beautiful. However, there are some faux bronze products that are less costly but may not have the same high quality. Brass, while elegant, is quick to form oxidation and acquire a green cast to it.

Back in the nineteenth century, before the days of parks and recreational areas, cemeteries were common meeting grounds for family gatherings. It was a popular picnicking spot, and therefore, not a morbid occasion. Many times, it was a way of including the dearly departed in family festivities since that was where they felt closest to their ancestors. Over the years it even became a peaceful place where couples could be fairly sure they could spend some quiet time together. For others of us, it was the place we learned to drive. My teacher, a good friend, was confident "I couldn't hurt anyone there".

Nowadays, it is very common to use the various lanes and paths for walking trails, taking advantage of the kind of terrain we want to challenge us. As long as it is done in a respectful manor, I am sure the deceased are glad to see us utilizing it. They know they are not forgotten.

In the process, we are able to educate ourselves from an historical and genealogical standpoint, if we are aware of what to look for. As someone who frequents cemeteries regularly, I can tell you, you never know whom you'll meet on a quest for their own heritage.

Understanding Symbolism in Cemeteries

A cemetery can be a treasure trove of clues to a person's lifetime, if you understand the symbolism used in days gone by. Present day monuments are often easier to read because we are familiar with the traditions of our times. While symbolism varies widely with individual preferences, here are some general meanings of the symbolism on headstones common in eras we may not be as familiar with.

Urn = the essence of life/their mortal remains -- was used a lot in Victorian times
Flame = eternal life
An anchor, (possibly over a Bible) = this soul was anchored in God and his word.
Masonic symbol = compass and square
3-link chain = symbol of Odd Fellows organization
Chain with broken link = member of the family is gone; with a finger pointing up to it usually meant that they were the last in that family line.
Plant, leaf or flowers = new life
A broken off or dead plant = life cut short in its peak
Flower bud = child or young person
Fully opened flower/rose = theirs was a life in full bloom
Lamb = usually used for an infant or child
Trimmed tree stone = a life cut off
Pillar = was the strength of the family and/or a pillar of the community.

Rough or partially unfinished stone = a life left unfinished

Books = a person's story, book of life, Bible

Open book = life is open to inspection

Closed book or stack of books atop stone = end of the story

Pen laying on book = the rest is unwritten, end of story

Doves = symbol of the Holy Spirit/the Trinity--- taking the spirit of the deceased to heaven.

Old cut or pruned tree trunk made of bronze, brass, cast iron or marble = a life cut down

Weeping willow tree = death/weeping and mourning

Hand with a finger pointing up = soul went to heaven

Hand with a finger pointing down (no, it's not what you think) = was the hand of God saying "I want you now", meaning that they hadn't lived very long.

Handshake = person holding hand on the right passed first, welcoming the other. If one sleeve was masculine and one feminine, whoever was on the right was welcoming the other. If the sleeves were the same—it was God welcoming the soul.

Rays of heaven = may the favor of the Lord shine upon you.

Curtains, often with tassels or gates = used primarily in Victorian times – open/means this person has passed from this life into the next world—closed/it is finished.

Book atop a pulpit or speaker style stone = sermon is over; the book is closed.

Scrollwork = used extensively for decoration in Victorian times.

Crown = symbolic of a heavenly reward representing any of the five crowns awarded a person for their life of service as promised in the Christian Bible. –The crowns and where the promises are found include:

Victory--1Corinth. Ch. 9:25
Life--Revelations Ch. 2:10
Glory --1Peter Ch. 5:2-4
Righteousness—2 Timothy Ch. 4:8
Rejoicing—1Thess. Ch.2: 19-20

*****

Chapter Seven

NETWORKING

One of the most fun ways to obtain information is by networking. Somewhere, someone out there knows something about someone you are researching. It is still important that you make every effort to verify anything you find with legal documentation. However, what you learn will add a new dimension to your heritage journals that you would not otherwise have. It is the human-interest stories that make it real and make those ancestors come to life.

Posting Queries

You don't have to wait until you reach a dead end in your research to post a query. In fact, it should probably be one of our first resources rather than a last resort. A "query" is a message that tells other people which family lines you are researching. It is the best way to help each other save time by sharing information. Too often we delay doing any research simply because we just don't have the time to go from one place to another to follow up on leads. Twenty years ago, I was intrigued by the idea of researching the past, but pressures of working and raising a family just didn't leave the spare time to pursue it. If I had simply looked in some of the right places and talked to the right people, I would have found information that had already been researched and shared by others.

So the first place to look is within the family. You might be surprised to learn that someone in the family has already done some, and maybe even extensive research on the family tree. They are usually very willing to share what they have by pointing you in the direction of where they obtained their information or maybe even making copies for you. However, don't be surprised if every once in a while you come across someone who is not generous with information.

The next place to look to posting queries is in local newspapers and genealogical society newsletters. Try to do this in the areas they may have lived. Someone may have already posted information in these papers/newsletters, and if so, subscribers to the newsletters will see your postings.

Another place to post queries is online electronic bulletin boards and message boards. Some online service providers offer genealogy forums where you can post these messages, and of course, it has the potential to reach a much wider audience.

You might also consider filling in the forms provided on Family Tree Maker Online. Just be sure to read the directions provided and don't forget to check for the names you are researching. Someone may have already posted information on the persons you are researching. Again, check alternative spellings. Many times over the years, letters get added or dropped from surnames, making them a little harder to find. You can then post your own queries.

Prepare to post your query by assembling the pertinent information you have and then writing down the questions that you still need answers to. You can make it a general query asking for more information on an entire branch of the family. However, you will want to include as much information as you know, to assure it is the right family and not just a family with the same last name. Another alternative is to make it a more specific query; for example, asking for anyone who may have known the names of your subject's parents, children or siblings, etc.

Queries may not always be about a particular person, but could be about a business or industry or about the local history of the area you are searching in. For example, you may wish to get information on thc local glass industry or the different job options within the industry that your ancestors worked. Sure, you can get information from the Internet, but it won't have the personal element we want to record. Somewhere, someone knows about the operations of it. They may have even known the subject of your research. Another example: You may wish to seek the location of an old family cemetery, perhaps an old coal mine or who owned it, maybe first families in a local church or founding families in a village. Some of this information can be at local libraries and genealogical societies. However, you may not find as much in the way of human-interest stories there, as you can from a public forum, interacting with others.

Next, no matter what form of query you do, be sure to remember to include names, date ranges, locations, and of course, your contact information in whatever form you prefer. It can be just your first name and phone number, a mailing address, and/or email address. Keep in mind, however, those who may read it or have the information, may not have or use email access, therefore a phone number could be important.

Getting & Staying Motivated

There are times when life and the everyday demands of jobs and family get us off track. Work responsibilities can take over our lives. A lot of the household chores simply have to be done eventually. However, sometimes all it takes is a good lead, either verbally from someone's story we hadn't previously heard, or running across a document or written detail that was previously unknown.

Nothing is more motivating when it comes to researching than having someone relate to you stories that they lived through. It inspires you to want to keep learning more until you have a complete picture. Ideally, get the story from more than one person's perspective. Each person will have their own unique twist to it, depending on how they perceived it, their state of mind at the time, and the emotions they were feeling then. For example, ask a grandparent or even an aunt or uncle, if they are old enough, what they remember about the Great Depression. Ask where they were at the time, and how it affected them. You will be surprised at the similarities and the differences. For a more personal note, another topic they will most certainly have fond memories of and that they may be willing to share is how, when and where they met and married their spouse. That can be quite a story in and of itself. One story will lead to another and before you know it, you won't be able to write fast enough to record all the details you will find so fascinating.

Even If you only consider it a hobby, try to set aside at least a little time for it in some capacity each week. It can be spent organizing your information, researching documents at the library or genealogy society, interviewing relatives, or networking and sharing information with other family historians. Staying on track is easier when we take it a step at a time and do it consistently. However, make interviewing and networking with others a priority, since time waits for no one.

Who to Interview

It isn't just about listing the names, dates and places. While facts are important, it is equally important to tell the story of how, why and where the subjects of your research, came to settle there. The human-interest stories we obtain will give us the biggest insight into who our ancestors were and how they lived their lives. They aren't just characters in a novel. They were real life folks that had ideas, emotions, and ethical (or unethical) values.

But where do we get this information? Besides all the literary resources and all the clues we find around our own homes (or those of relatives) that have been previously mentioned, there is another very valuable source of information. That is from the people we interview.

Before making the contact, go over again what you do know to find out what facts are still missing. Make a list of questions on missing information, and then match them with a list of persons who may have been witness to what you need to know, such as their family members, friends, neighbors, employers, co-workers, church or organization members. Sometimes those you least expect are the ones that have the answers you seek.

Pay special attention to dates to establish a time frame, and places, so that you know where you might search as far as community, city, county, state, or foreign country. Should you feel you have reached a dead end with literary sources, it is time to research from the human perspective. This really is the fun part of genealogy. You'll usually find that most of those you ask are very willing to share their memories. There may be a few who wish not to and we have to respect their privacy. The subject of family secrets generates a lot of controversy, so we will address that in another chapter.

You will obtain family legends, stories and traditions that can extend your family history back in time over several centuries. However, keep in mind that some of these stories could be distorted having been passed down through the generations. Somewhere in there, though, are details that are probably based in fact. It is our job to research both written and oral evidence and document it through other sources, before adding it as truth to our recorded family legacy. Be sure to note your source, or at least that it was obtained through an interview and may not be able to be documented.

Go prepared with whatever tools are at your disposal, such as an I-pad, Netbook or laptop, a camera, video recorder, and/or tape recorder (if the respondent doesn't mind being taped), and of course, a notebook. Take along any pictures you have to show them. They just may be able to identify the people in the older photos. Record any stories they tell you, because you probably won't be able to write or type fast enough. This gives you the opportunity to go back to it for further reference. Most of the facts can be verified with legal documents later. When interviewing, the camera is very important, in case there are people or places you'd like to photograph for further documentation.

Interviewing Our Elders

Unfortunately, relationships are sometimes put on the back burner, because everyone is busy and time goes by. The longer we wait the more their memory fades, if we don't make an effort to get it recorded now. All too soon, the time comes when it's too late to ask the questions we wanted to ask or visit the people we wanted to know better.

Grandma knew what she was talking about when she said, "It'll still be there when you're dead and gone". She couldn't have put it any plainer that what we think matters, matters little in the overall scheme of things. It is the quality time we spend with others that lasts and teaches us life's lessons.

I cannot stress enough, the importance of not putting off getting to know extended family and interviewing them now as to their perspective on the family heritage. Many of them have forgotten more than we ever knew about our own lineage. With a little memory jogging and the right questions, it is amazing what comes back to them.

Who should we ask for information? It is best to start with your parent's oldest living relatives. If their health is stable, they are sure to enjoy your visit.

What should you ask? This is largely determined by what you already know and what you still need to know to put the pieces together. Although other topics are discussed in greater detail in other chapters, here are some recommended topics to help you get started:

1. Ask them about themselves and their immediate family first so that you can add it to your generational charts of names, the dates, marriages and children. Even if they don't know or remember facts, they are likely to be able to tell you who may know or where to look.
2. What do they remember about their parents and siblings and include factual data as well as the human-interest stories.
3. Where were they living and attending school?
4. Discover how and where they met and married their spouse.
5. Describe their life, if they lived through the Great Depression.
6. Ask them to describe a particular relative's personality or their relationship with them.
7. Don't forget to ask about military and career choices.

8. Go back as far as they can remember to find out if they knew anything about where their ancestors came from and why they located where they did.
9. Another real memory jogger is to ask about the most important events that they can remember in their lives.
10. By all means, remember to ask them to recount the funniest things that ever happened to them to inject a little humor. It makes for great human- interest stories.
11. Likewise, have them describe their most embarrassing moments.

There are countless other topics you can cover and one visit will probably not be enough. You need not worry yet about putting all your notes in the proper journal/album format. For now, just get the information and you can organize it as time permits.

Interviewing Siblings

If you are lucky enough to have siblings in your life, don't let another day go by without doing something to build your relationship with them. In what we might call the natural order of life, the day will come when our parents are gone and our siblings, be they biological or adopted, are our only connection to the past. Of course, if we have children, we want to be sure to pass that past onto them.

When you already have a good relationship with your siblings and see them often, then you have probably grown along with them into adulthood and know firsthand how they

have changed and matured throughout the years. You know
when and if you can count on them through it all, and that
they will be there for you no matter what. Talk with them
often about your lives as children for the purpose of
recording it. Be specific when you compare information on
family members, dates, vacations, special occasions, family
pets, etc. You might ask what their earliest memories were of
home and family. Be sure to recall the funny times you and
they can remember. You'll be surprised at how much their
perception of it differs from your own. They will also
remember things that you don't. This will help to build a
relationship with each other that is not only unique, but
priceless. What a great addition this exchange will make to
your journals or memory books. They may even have photos
that you weren't aware of or other memorabilia that you can
copy.

What if your siblings live out of town or out of state for
that matter? Of course, we live separate, distinct lives. That
is a normal part of growing up and we need not feel guilty for
the path our lives take. However, our memories were of
growing up together in the good times as well as the bad. We
knew the child in each other in a way no one else did.

Sometimes, with time and distance, we forget that as we
grow and mature, the essence in all of us changes, that is, the
person we are, and what we are about. Our beliefs, priorities,
and values may change. Even though we may love each
other very much, the distance can be a factor and we may not
have the opportunity to discuss it with each other very often.

Some siblings may lose track of each other and think of
that person as they knew them "when". There may even have
been misunderstandings and one or the other of you may not

feel comfortable sharing your lives now. But in the end, we will all know it doesn't matter and that we were all here to learn from each other. In fact, we truly are "all one".

Another thing to remember is that once they are gone, there will be a hundred things you wish you had told them and a hundred things you wish you had asked them. It's much better to do it now and there won't be any regrets. There is one thing on this subject that I feel strongly about. That is, "siblings" are God's gift to us so that when our parents are gone, we are not alone on this earth plane. Our children will grow up and move on to lead lives of their own, just as nieces and nephews do. It is siblings who are there for each other through it all. If you are an only child, perhaps you were given close friends or cousins who are "like a brother or sister" to you.

Even if your parents are no longer living, perhaps some of their brothers and sisters are. You can apply the above ideas for discussing with them to learn about their lives and that of your parents as they grew up. There is a wealth of information just waiting to be discovered that will give you a glimpse into what life was like, especially during the depression. Best of all, you'll probably uncover some new information to give you new leads on where you might search next. You just might be amazed at what local history may emerge during your search. Again, for some things to be sure to cover:

1. Have them give you any details you are missing on themselves, their spouse and their children and grandchildren.

2. Inquire about their memories of their own parents and any siblings.

3. Get their perspective of the neighborhood they and/or you lived in, as well as school experiences.

4. Have them relate stories of how and when they met and married their spouse.

Also see questions 5 through 10 for "Interviewing Elders", as they apply.

Because of the very nature of our subject matter, you may find some of the material (or in similar wording) on topics listed in more than one chapter in this book. However, because of its importance, it bears repeating.

Making Connections

All through life we make connections; ones that begin when we are born and others that we find along our journey. There are those who come into our lives and stay for just a short time, but leave a lasting impact on our hearts. Then there are those that will remain with us for the rest of our lives. Of course, there are those that we may feel we could have done without, but they too, had a purpose in our life. No matter what type of connection we may have, it has a predetermined purpose in perfecting our souls. Sometimes people have a way of walking in and out of our lives. We might call these people "acquaintances" that cross our paths, maybe only once in a lifetime, or that we may only run into occasionally. It is probable that we learn something, either positive or negative from each one of them.

But what impact do these "connections" have on our genealogy research? I can tell you first hand that they make all the difference in the world. Even though immediate and extended family members are some of our best resources for information, you will be amazed at what you will learn from distant relatives or even total strangers who walk into your life for one reason or another. Not only do they offer a whole new perspective, they will undoubtedly have data and perhaps even a photo or two that you don't have. The common availability of copiers and scanners make the probability of their sharing them much more likely.

Chances are very good that there is at least one family member (and most likely more than one) in any given family that has already done some or even extensive research into the family history. You will never know that until you begin asking around. On the other hand, you could have information they don't have. Getting and keeping in contact with each other will not only help you to share the wealth of information and photos, but you could begin building a relationship with relatives you didn't know even existed. You may find that they are as enthusiastic as you are about your research and that there are all manner of things you can investigate together. Again, it is a lot like being your own detective.

How to locate distant relatives? Assuming you have some leads to go on as far as surnames, and can get to Internet access, go to as many of the ancestry/heritage message boards as you can. List whom you are searching for information on and your contact information. In addition, you might visit any of the free white pages phone directory listings and do a search in the last known area for persons with that surname. In this way, you can check with them to see if they know whom you may be seeking information on. Be sure you identify yourself and how you may be connected to the person you are researching. Let them know that it is purely for genealogy purposes, and they may be more inclined to be of help. Although they may not have the information themselves, they can probably refer you to who might be their family historian. Talking with that person might be your next terrific lead.

When you get a contact, how you wish to proceed is, of course, up to the two of you. It may be by phone, email or visit. First you'll need to verify that this is the right person you are seeking information about. For example, a lot of people shared common names many years ago. Names were not as unique and individual as they seem to be today, and very often you had to rely on your middle initial to distinguish between other persons. It seems everyone had a John, Mary, Anna, etc. in each generation. To make it more complicated, they often married someone with the same names in their family. It was also the norm to name children after their father or mother, which could become quite confusing. For that reason, nicknames became very handy.

Once you are satisfied that the subject is indeed the person you are seeking information about, please be considerate of your informant's time. Always ask permission to identify your source in your journaling either by name or as a friend or relative interviewed. I cannot stress how important it is to interview as many as possible that may have known the subject of your search. I, personally, have interviewed distant relatives from two weeks to a few months before their unexpected passings. It isn't just elders we need to be asking questions of. Talk to siblings, cousins, aunts and uncles NOW while memories and details are fresher in their minds, and record them.

*****

Chapter Eight

HANDLING SENSITIVE INFORMATION

Changes & Confidentiality

Once we realize that life is all about change, not only does it help to free us from worry, but opens the door to help us plan for the future. Either we can go kicking and screaming into the next phase of our life or we can make the very most of it. But however we choose, we will go, because life is supposed to change.

How does that apply to the quest to find our heritage? It would seem that one has nothing to do with the other. However, as we research, we will find out how our ancestors accepted changes in their lives. Those who did not were more likely to experience difficulties and strife throughout their lives, while those who did "go with the flow", so to speak, were able to use the experience for the greater good. It may be difficult at times to discern what that good is, but we don't necessarily need to know that now, only that in the bigger scheme of things, it will eventually be revealed. Of course we will make some bad choices, just as our ancestors made mistakes. The whole idea is that we always try to do the best we can and learn from our mistakes. After all, we have free will.

It is also very possible as we research, that we will learn a lot from their choices as well as our own. This is where we may uncover little known facts that they likely would have preferred not been made known. However, even though they are gone, there may be things that come to light that others could eventually need to know. While we want to be sensitive as to how it may affect others, things such as previous marriages, adoptions, criminal records, and physical or mental illnesses could be situations that have a profound effect in understanding and dealing with our own current problems.

Just like those who have gone before us, there may also be things we don't particularly want made known while we are alive. If this is information that would be helpful to someone else or to subsequent descendants, please consider making note of it somewhere for them to know where to find it. You can always put the documentation, along with a personal note explaining anything you need to tell them, in a sealed envelope. For safekeeping, either literally put it in your safe, give to your attorney, or put it in a safe place so that loved ones can easily find it. As a matter of fact, leaving a letter/note for each of your immediate family members upon your death would be something they would cherish for a lifetime.

The old adage that time heals all things is true in the sense that it makes it easier to bear. Not that we forget, but that we learn ways to cope, deal with changes and losses, and use them for the greater good of all.

Family Secrets

While you are researching your family history, you will no doubt uncover some family secrets. It would be extremely rare for a family to be able to say that there have never been any secrets somewhere in their family lineage. Dealing with sensitive information can be a touchy subject. For past generations, there was indeed a social and moral stigma attached to illegitimacy. Therefore, illegitimacies and adoptions were some of the most commonly held family secrets. Children "born out of wedlock", as it was referred to, and the corresponding adoptions may have been just as common in previous generations. In years gone by, it was usually kept hidden for as long as possible, where as now, it is very common for a woman to be a single parent without social repercussions.

However, somehow, somewhere, someday, the truth always has a way of coming out. Is it better to deal with it now, or risk having it come out at an inopportune time and cause more problems by affecting many more lives?

There is a saying that the two most precious gifts that you can give a child, besides love, are roots and wings. This topic may very well evoke strong emotions on both sides of the debate. There are different schools of thought on whether or not children and biological parents would want to know about each other. After interviewing numerous subjects on both sides of the debate, it is clear that it can become a very complex situation, especially when these secrets involve innocent parties such as spouses, and unknown siblings.

Some believe that the parents who raise the child are their "real" parents. Most will agree that having them can be the easy part and that raising them is the hardest part of being a parent. True, you may biologically have a child, but that doesn't mean you are able to nurture that child. There could be all kinds of reasons why a parent is unable to nurture a child. They could be physically, emotionally or financially unable to do so, and it usually has nothing at all to do with not loving the child. Of course, there are always exceptions to every rule. It is now believed that children have the right, and often demand to know, their genetic roots.

However, parents who take in a child are "choosing" that child. That child can always take comfort in knowing that they were "specially" chosen. There has to be a special place in heaven for those parents who take on the pleasures and responsibilities of nurturing a child of their own choosing.

Biologically speaking, knowing about adoption can be vital if a physical ailment should manifest itself sometime in their future. It could literally mean the difference in survival and/or our quality of life. With all of today's medical marvels, we would still need a match if we were to need bone marrow, tissue or organs to restore our health. Our very best chance of finding a match, are generally those in our immediate family. Aside from medical reasons, you may wonder what difference it makes. As we get older, we find we lose relatives at an alarming rate. It may seem to some that there is no one left who cares. Won't it be great to know that there is a large extended family?

To Know or Not to Know

Ideally, an adopted child can be blessed with two families, their biological and their adopted family. Whenever all parties agree to work together for the good of the children, miracles can and do happen. Families who can blend together, understand their respective roles, and yet, give the other side the respect they need, have accomplished one of the most challenging aspects of parenthood they will ever face.

However, because we are human, it is not always possible for it to go as smoothly as we would like. Particularly when spouses and other siblings are involved, it can become quite complicated. Lives can be disrupted because of indiscretions. Egos and emotions are involved, and feelings are hurt. Forgiveness is not always as easy as we are led to believe it should be. Misunderstandings can cloud our rationality. Adults must remember to put the welfare of the child before their own interests and desires.

Laws vary from state to state as to what age and under what circumstances a child may seek information on their lineage before their adoption. Some adoptive parents will gladly share all the information they have with their adopted child on their biological lineage. Of course, those are the starting points. There are also national registries online that you can register your information on and periodically check back to see if anyone is looking for you. These are generally a good idea, because it helps to protect those who do not wish to know or be found.

Children—Sometimes the adopted, be they children or now adults, are perfectly happy not knowing and do not wish to pursue it. That is their choice and needs to be respected. Still others wish to claim their right to know, as they reach an age at which they can legally obtain information. They want to know who they were, why their biological parents were unable to be involved in their lives, if they have siblings, their medical history, their biological lineage and/or their family history. This is in no way a reflection on the parents who raised them, and it certainly does not mean they do not love their adopted parents. Still others seek to build relationships with their biological family. They need to be prepared for the possibility that they may be disappointed, if their enthusiasm is not returned.

Parents---Circumstances in a biological parent's life may have changed dramatically since the time of the adoption. They could be afraid that contact with them would be a disruption of the child's life, if they were to become involved with them now. If a parent does not wish to be found, it can also mean that they are still not able to assume an active role and/or believe that the child is better off without them in their lives. We have to respect that decision because that very well could be the case. Adoptive parents can best be supportive of the child by assisting them as much as they can. They can also let the children know they are there for them unconditionally, no matter what the outcome. In the final analysis, each situation is unique and all parties involved need to remember that children come into this world innocent. Children depend on adults to do what is right for them.

Of all those interviewed, the general contention is that they would want to know. Whether or not they wish to expand on that information now or at sometime in the future is their choice. That decision does not have to be made immediately, but at least they have that option available.

The children who choose not to pursue it may do so for any number of reasons. There could be a fear that it will compromise their time. Perhaps they do not want to risk being disappointed if it is found that the interest is not returned. Finding negative information about their biological family may also be a concern. Some are just perfectly happy with the blessings they have. Others just plain do not wish to know their biological roots for fear of hurting the feelings of their adopted family. Still some might prefer to research their adopted roots, and that is fine. That too, is their right.

*****

Once we have uncovered the previously unknown details of our ancestor's lives, we need, of course, to work to verify them through recorded legal documents. It helps if we can understand why actual facts were kept secret to begin with. For example, many foreigners who came to the United States around the turn of the century did so because of religious persecution or political upheavals in their "old country".

Sometimes other information can be viewed as sensitive and there are those who feel that it is inappropriate to record it. This can be anything from indiscretions to causes of death or derogatory comments made about them by others. Upon further examination, there is a good chance you will find that what might have been considered a derogatory remark by outsiders, may have actually been a precious memory of a loved one. For that very reason, it needs to be recorded. It may also involve cases of incarceration (public court dockets are helpful in this regard) or mental illness. Some may request that so called "secrets" never be revealed or at least not until after their own passing. We must be sensitive to the feelings of others while attempting to preserve our history.

For ways of preserving these family secrets, please refer to details in Chapter Ten.

*****

Chapter Nine

JOURNALING

Factual Data Journal
vs. the Memory Journal

One of the first things you will need to decide is the format of your journaling. If you are a person who likes to stick to just the facts and as many of them as you can find, this type of journal is for you. You will need a good sturdy binder that is expandable because you will need plenty of room for adding pages. You will be adding pages for each member of the family in each generation and for each side of the family, so it can get pretty thick.

Be sure you have some good generational (showing the lineage of descendants) charts as well as family charts. Generational charts contain basic data such as full name, date and place of birth, marriage date and to whom, date of death and sometimes place of burial. They begin with you and go back generations through grandparents, great-grandparents and so on. Siblings are generally not shown on these, but on family charts. You will need extra copies of family charts in order to profile each family member, their specific data and their descendants through the years. There are a variety of different formats available to choose from on most genealogy websites that are free for the downloading. You may also be able to find some at your local library or genealogy society. Choose what works best for you or use them to create your own. You may modify it so that it reflects the information you want to save along with space for any notations you want to make. It is also recommended that you get a package or more of plastic page protectors to insert your pages to keep them from getting dirty or torn. Again, always use pencil for ease of change.

To "journal" means to write, anything from a record of the past to memoirs for reflection. Choose any format you like. They can contain the above data pages, but the emphasis is usually on the memories and stories handed down from one generation to another. A journal is usually handwritten in a bound book form, but can be done on the computer and entered into a binder for ease of access should you choose to make changes later.

In my experience, some of the best journals turn out to be a combination of the two. It certainly would have been a treasure, had our ancestors had the foresight to write down their thoughts, as well as the facts. Most entries were only found within their Bibles and of course, there was not much space to make any personal comments. What a difference it would have made to our family histories. Let's record it now for our descendants as a gift to treasure.

Get some nice covered journals or even just several notebooks. Keep your notebooks or journals handy near your chair or any place you will have easy access so that you can jot down things as they come to mind, or pick it up and write whenever you have a few minutes. It doesn't matter right now if it is in any particular order. Again, the important thing is to get it written down. Eventually, you can organize your writing into chapters or other formats. Always include at least an approximate date at the top of the page. Think of it as a kind of diary, only instead of just a daily entry, it is more of an on-going story. You may eventually want to enter any or all of your content into your computer Word program for backup or to put on a disc or flash drive.

The best of journals record memories of both the joys and sorrows in the lives of those we write about. It is all a part of our history and our life. Recording it not only tells others who our loved ones were, but also will allow insight into the person we have become by knowing them.

Following are some of the different kinds of memory journals to consider creating. They can serve as a great reference point for several aspects of our research.

Another kind of journaling involves combining your journaling (the written record, that includes the facts) with your preservation method, such as albums, memory books, etc. It can often also include adding photos and memorabilia of the event or subject. An example of this would be creating a wedding album/journal or a school days album. See Chapter Eleven on "Preserving our heritage".

Create a Timeline Diary

What is a timeline diary? It is an abbreviated version of our history with the primary focus on the chronological time periods. Basically, it is recording specific significant dates and/or events in our lives or the lives of others that have affected or influenced us, be they personal, local or national.

Start now with the present and work backwards. Although you will also do this in a "From This Day Forward" journal, our primary focus here is in creating one for the past. This one will be a valuable resource used for referencing the time frames of the past, and how they relate to the present.

Without computer access, just record it in a notebook. With the computer, it is much easier to use a word program to add new information as it becomes available, make changes to existing facts, and for keeping data in chronological order.

There are both positive and negative events that bear recording, such as births, deaths, promotions, layoffs, trips, moving, new cars, other major purchases, etc. This makes for easy reference without looking up receipts, certificates, and so forth, at a time when you may need to know. Once you get in the habit of noting these events, it will be automatic to do so. As you start a new calendar year, literally use your calendar to record these significant moments. You can than copy it from your calendar into a timeline file on your computer. If you have already used your present calendar to jog the memory and have saved no previous calendars that you can use as reference, (and your memory fails you), then you may have to spend a little time and go through personal information that you have kept over the years. The good news is, you should only have to do it once in order to have a list of pertinent information for quick reference.

Therefore, the major purpose for a timeline diary, as it relates to genealogy research, will be to give you dates to use as reference in looking for clues. For example, you may know your grandfather was born in the United Sates in a particular month and year say, April 1893, then you know he won't be listed in the 1890 Federal census or as an immigrant in 1900, which is why timelines are important to our research. Or it could also tell us in what years certain family members attended high school or a particular school. That is important if you are looking for information on their school days.

By the way, don't worry if you don't have the specific date of the month. In some cases, the month and year are sufficient. Not only will this information assist us in researching our ancestry, it can help us out in the present as well. Obviously, you will then know at a glance, how long you had a particular job, home, vehicle etc. This could come in handy when it comes to filling out an application, writing a resume, applying for a loan, checking warranty information, and countless other situations that arise, without having to go digging for the information.

*****

Chapter Ten

TYPES OF JOURNALS

From This Day Forward Journals

This is probably one of the easiest to create. It is different from a timeline diary of the past in the fact that, not only will it record date sequences of events, but will describe future entries in detail. That is because you are working from this day forward to record life as it unfolds, along with traditions and countless incidents that arise. It is similar to a diary, but much more in depth. By journaling this, you will have accumulated a history that is irreplaceable for future generations.

Obviously, no one will be able to do all of the ideas provided here, so pick and choose those you like or that will work best for you, given the kind of keepsake you choose to create. Start with a nice covered journal or even just a notebook. Remember, you can always organize it into a different format at a later date. You need not worry about putting it in any particular order, because you are mainly concerned with recording events as they come to mind, just as you would when writing in a diary.

Begin with the present year while events are fresh in your mind. Even if a year is more than half gone, it isn't too late to record memorable events. When you have trouble remembering, just refer to your entries on your calendar to refresh your memory.

Why do this? We are usually concerned with researching our ancestors, forgetting that we ARE the ancestors of the future generations. It will be immensely helpful for them, or you, to refer to it in the future. It might be similar to a daily diary that just records the highlights of each year, both good and bad. In this case, it doesn't just serve to remind us of what we lived through, but could also be of use providing timeline and details should there be medical or legal questions we need answers to in the future. It doesn't need to be lengthy unless you wish to record it in more detail. If so, be sure to include any thoughts and feelings that come to mind, as well.

How to do this? Use whichever method you prefer that works well for you. Option one might be to use a notebook. Option two, another preferred alternative, may be to use loose leaf and a soft binder with dividers for the years. Add a page for each category used and add pages as needed. Use the categories that apply to you. Even if you don't use them all, some are better than none. Page categories to consider including for each year might be:

Family/friend births: Record dates, parents, and any specifics you wish to recall.

Deaths/funerals attended of family or friends: Include dates, cause, location, place of burial, other specific details.

Travels: Places visited, dates, best highlights, trials and tribulations, etc.

Major purchases that year: This one doesn't help too much with your genealogy research, unless it's to give an example of your lifestyle. However, it is a good place to keep a record of how long you have had specific autos, furniture, appliances, done major remodeling, etc.

Medical procedures of household members, immediate or even extended family members: Include approximate dates, diagnosis, etc.

Financial: Include gains and losses, approximate dates, sources, amounts, and any other pertinent information. (This can help at tax time).

Self-improvement: What did I do during the year to improve my physical condition, my self-esteem, my mental attitude, my education, even my circumstances?

Recreation: Besides any travel, what interests or hobbies did I, or household members pursue? How about clubs or organizations?

Changes: Record here any changes to your lifestyle that have occurred including any firsts, as well as moves by you or others close to you. Include when, where and how it may have affected you. Include what new people have entered your life with some regularity, for whatever reason.

Spiritual growth: As we get older, we realize that this is one of the most important categories. Have we accomplished all that we were meant to do? What have we done during the year to be of service to others? Has it been merely financial support or did we become involved, giving of our time and talents?

Individual Personal Journals

Obviously, these are done on a particular topic in which you want to expand and show greater detail. You can create one on any topic that is near and dear to your heart. A few ideas:
  --Wedding journal
  --Family traditions and/or holiday journal
  --Family reunions journal
  --Travel/vacations journal
  --School days journal
  --Pets we have had over our lifetime journal
  --Homes/places we have lived journal
  --A favorite family recipes journal
  --A tribute to a specific person (friend or relative)
  --A tribute to mom or dad (makes a great Mother's Day or Father's Day gift.)

For the mother's or father's tribute, consider including these things about them that touched your life, such as:
  --What were your earliest memories of them?
  --Where were you living? Be sure to write down the addresses of the places you remember living at growing up. What do you remember about life at those places? (You can expand on this later with any indoor or outdoor photos you discover).

--What physical characteristics and personality traits did you inherit from them? What was/is their height, hair and eye color?

--What was their favorite color and why?

--What did they like to do in their spare time?

--What personality traits do they have?

--What hopes and dreams did they have for themselves?

 --Expand on any special events in their lives. What memories of it did they share with you?

--What were their favorite foods and did they have any favorite recipes? (These could also be included in a special heirloom recipe book.)

--Did they have any special little sayings that come to mind?

--What smells, sights or sounds remind you of them?

--What kinds of education did they have?

--Were they in the military? What memories of it did they share with you?

--Where were they employed? List as many of these places of employment as you can along with their job description and any memories they may have shared with you of their work experience.

--What did they value most in their lives?

--What were their spiritual/moral values?

--What hopes and dreams did they have for you and any siblings?

--Were they strict or lenient?

--What did you choose to do different with your own family?

--What did they like to do for fun?

--Where did they like to vacation?

--What memories do you have of special vacations with them?

--What memories of their parents or other ancestors did they share with you?

--What memories of their own childhoods did they share with you?

--What funny little stories were handed down from previous generations?

--What funny things happened with them that you would like to pass down?

--What most embarrassing moments do you recall with them?

--What were the most important things they taught you?

--Was there ever any special advice that they gave you?

--What other things come to mind that you learned from them, either through word or example, such as honesty, integrity, spirituality, hunting, golfing, fishing, cooking, work ethics, etc.

--If they are gone, what special time did you share with them at the end?

--If you didn't have that opportunity, what would you have said?

--This next one is heavy, but in retrospect, if you could change anything, what would you have changed in your relationship with them?

The best of journals record both the joys and sorrows of your memories. It is all a part of our history and our life.
Recording it not only tells others who our loved ones were

but also offers insight into the person we have become by knowing them.

Past Memory Journals

Take note, this differs from your memoirs in the fact that, a memoir is more of an autobiography profiling your own life. (Forward journals can assist with your memoirs.) Whereas, what we are attempting to do with genealogy research is to focus on our ancestors.

Again, keep your notebooks handy for jotting down your memories as you think of them or for writing whenever you have spare moments. It can be as basic or as detailed as you would like. On each page, make sure there is an approximate date that the event took place. Write about one family tradition or event in your family at a time. Include as much detail as you can remember. You can always add to it as you think about the past. Even if you only write a few minutes at a time, after a while, you will have accumulated a family history.

Some years are more memorable than others. There will be times when you don't recall anything significant. Other years are so etched in our memories that we certainly don't need a calendar to remind us of a crisis or traumatic event, the joys and sorrows, losses, births, medical emergencies or diagnosis, travels, and the list goes on.

Do a review of the following topics in the previous journal list and choose those to write on that apply to the type of journal you are doing or that are most important to you.

Any one of these topics listed could become a journal of its own, but for a collective past memories type of journal, here are some additional topics to contemplate and consider including in your journals (ideally, for each person):

Thinking about each of your parents---grandparents--- siblings---aunts and uncles--Review the previous list of suggested questions under a mother or father tribute in the Individual Personal Journals section. Apply those questions to each person in order to get a better look at their individual lives.

About us---In addition to any of the aforementioned questions that apply, be sure to include:
--What were the most embarrassing things that have ever happened to you?
--What do you consider to be the dumbest things you ever did and what did you learn from them?
--Excluding professional comedy, what are the funniest things that you have ever witnessed over the years?
--What are you most proud of accomplishing in life?
--Have you ever had a supernatural or unexplained experience or know someone who did?
--You've heard the expression, "Regrets, I've had a few". If you could go back and make a change, what would it be?

Careers---
--List the years and places you have been employed
--Your job description
--Your likes and dislikes about the job

--Your bosses/supervisors at that job
--Those who were your closest friends at that particular
jobsite
--And maybe those who weren't that may have made an
impression.
--Be sure to include military service.

Our children---
A chapter for each child that can include a page for each
topic, such as:
--Personal attributes like hair and eye color and whom
they looked like
--How you chose their name
--What was significant about the day they were born?
Ex: The weather, what events were going on in the
world at that time, and where you were living, etc.
--There may also be more personal information you wish
to include such as your feelings at the time, length of
labor, first reactions of parents and other family
members upon their arrival, things that you might have
recorded in a baby book, such as first tooth, first steps,
etc. Don't forget to include all the funny incidents or
things they have said or done that you can remember
over the years.
--To give insight into what they were like then, include a
list of their favorites as they were growing up, such as
colors, foods, games to play, toys, playmates, favorite
TV programs and cartoon characters, any special
birthday celebrations and include what made them so
special.

--A list of as many of their teachers as can be remembered, including who were their favorites and why.

--The highlights of their high school years, their best friends throughout school, the clubs or organizations they belonged to, their accomplishments, those they dated through high school and brought home to meet you, and your impressions of them.

--Memories of their sporting events or other school activities they participated in, their college years and how you dealt with the empty nest.

Grandchildren---

For each grandchild, include most of the above with special emphasis on the funny things they have said and done, and how having them in your life has been a blessing.

This next set of topics could apply to either a forward or a past journal. These topics are not as important to our "heritage" to document, but they do add a fun aspect to our journals and will be interesting to look back on in years to come. They can become the human-interest stories handed down from one generation to another. So contemplate and write down some fun things. These are topics you may wish to include.

Pets--- They are usually part of our families, so it only makes sense to include them in our memory journals. Make a list of the pets we have had (or add for your future journals) as far back as we can remember.

--Their names, approximate ages, descriptions
--Their personality traits and what was the most special
about them. For some, this list can get quite lengthy.
--Don't forget to include how you came to get them
--How they exited your life

Hobbies and Interests---Looking back over the years, list
the things you have been interested in, or pursued in your
spare time.
--What or who got you interested?
--Who else enjoyed it with you?
--What drew you to it?
--Was it for fun or profit or both?

Cars---Remember your first car? Subsequent cars?
--The year, make, model and color.
--Why and where you got them and the price you paid.
--The time frame you acquired and how long you kept
them. Try to list as many as you can remember; some
will stand out as special and make a note as to why they
made you proud.

People in our lives who have influenced us---These are the
people who have helped to shape the person we have
become:
--Who they were and how they influenced us whether
positively or negatively. They can be parents, step
parents, foster or adoptive parents, grandparents,
children and grandchildren, in-laws, extended family,

pastors, teachers, employers, fellow employees, friends, neighbors, acquaintances, celebrities, the media, etc.
--Spiritual influences in our lives---The people who have either passed their faith on to us or reached out to us
--The experiences that have led us to a deeper understanding of our spirituality

Weddings---

--Include engagement and shower information you recall, such as dates, places and times
--Descriptions of wedding attire, flowers and décor used for the ceremony and the reception
--Descriptions of music for the ceremony and the reception
--Who officiated the ceremony, the bridal party and any other participants
--Be sure to include any traditions that were followed.
--This account would not be complete without including moments that stood out at both ceremony and reception, whether funny or not so funny, that will not soon be forgotten.

Homes/places we have lived--- In the beginning, a fun thing to do might be to include a page with an idea of what your dream home would be like, so you can see how you have progressed over the years. Next, list the places you have lived over the years. With each one, include:
--Approximate dates
--Addresses, if you remember them, and all who resided there.

--A description of the house/apartment interior, how many rooms, type of décor you remember, or lack of it (if you are really creative, you can even include a sketch of the floor plan, as you remember it).
--Describe the exterior of it and the yard/acreage
--What was special about the place? Ex. Happiest times there, big yard, etc.
--What fond memories do you have about each place?
--Include any available photos, if you wish, depending on the format you are choosing to save it in. Photos are also terrific, especially for insurance purposes in the event you should need to file a claim.

Vacations---Again, not a necessity for your "heritage", but they add fun human-interest stories. After all, some of our best memories are created when we are relaxed and "on vacation".

--List the places and dates and all who accompanied you.
--How did you get there?
--Was there anything memorable about the places you stayed?
--What sights did you see?
--Who did you visit?
--What was your favorite part of the trip?
--What activities did you participate in while you were there?
--What funny things happened while there?
--What would I want to see again?

Family traditions or events---On each page, make sure there is an approximate date that the event took place. Write about one family tradition or event in your family at a time. Include as much detail as you can remember.

School Memories

While the ideal time to start a journal of your child's school years is at the beginning of a new school year, it is never too late. It could be a journal, a pictorial record of the school year or a combination of both.

Again, it can be as simple as the bare facts or as detailed as you like. There are no set rules, therefore, these suggestions are meant to be ideas for what you might want to document. There are two ways you can approach this:

First, assemble it as a do-it-yourself project, which will make a terrific gift for them later. Furthermore, if you are going to do it yourself, asking certain questions of them could open the lines of communication. As months turn into years, before you know it, you have a documented history in words, as well as pictures that you can save or scrapbook for them.

Of course, you'll want to keep notes on the funny things that happen during the school year. You might even record their thoughts… and fears. It may be of help later, should problems arise.

Get some inexpensive notebooks. Begin with one for each child and add extras as needed. You might consider starting with school shopping, anything special you got for them, perhaps what you spent and photos, if available. Years later, they will be amazed at their taste in style and the trends of the times.

Next you will want to document that first day of school, since it is usually one of the biggest and busiest days in their young lives. Be sure to get photos of that one.

For younger children, you'll want to save some of the best samples of their artwork and keep in a file folder, at least until you are ready to place in an album or scrapbook. For older children, some of their best-saved homework or essays will work. If space does not allow you to keep all of the good ones, consider photographing and resizing them for using multiple ones on a page. Of course, progress reports, teacher notes and report cards are a must to file.

The second alternative is to use the process as a teaching tool, involving them in the creating process by showing them the fun and value of learning early journaling. This makes wonderful rainy day projects for them.

In high school, in addition to all of the day-to-day activities, be sure to document special activities, such as band, sports, proms, clubs, etc. By this age, if they have taken an interest in completing their journal, they will have saved memorabilia and made notes to use in it.

Graduation from high school is the culmination of their school years and the beginning of a new chapter in their lives, be it college or taking on adult responsibilities. The same journaling can be applied to those college years.

Whichever way you decide, be sure to include: Their favorite subjects, who their teachers were, who their friends were and are now, activities and any honors they receive.

What if your children are already well into their school years or grown and gone? You can still sort the previous information and photos for each child that you have and organize it into an album or journal. As you look through the data, jot down anything that comes to mind and journal it. You may or may not be able to remember much, but a little is better than nothing.

What if it's your own, a sibling's, or your parent's school life you want to explore and document? If all else fails, there are always class photos and yearbooks to obtain information and/or jog those memories. Don't forget to include the stories of their school days they have passed down to you.

On a special note here...you may wish to include some negative school experiences as well as the positive. Examples being: bad grades, trouble with teachers, or bullying. This allows descendants to understand the issues you have gone through that may have had a bearing on the forming of your personality. At the same time it lets them know how you handled it and if there was a particular outcome. You may also include what you learned from the experience.

Not for Women Only

It is true that most men often pay less attention to detail than women. However, men who remember the details and take the time to write them down, offer an invaluable perspective, that would not otherwise be noted. While women usually concentrate on the feelings and the emotional side of a memory, men are usually better at remembering the intellectual and factual side of the situation. Those two halves create a balance of the whole experience. They are both equally important.

Time is the one thing we all never seem to have enough of, especially while trying to meet the obligations of raising a family and earning a living. During that time, it is hard to imagine that we might ever reach the place where we wish we could remember the details we lived through, both good and bad that made us what we have become. However, if we can take just a minute to grab our notebook (you know, the one you keep by your favorite chair), and write them down now, it will be much easier to jog the memory later. The story from a man's perspective will make the story of your lineage even richer.

Some of the topics men may want to take special care to expand on are:

--As much of your childhood as you can remember, including things you collected when you were a child
--Sports highlights you participated in
--Who your friends were and the activities you enjoyed with them
--The trouble you may have gotten into, how you got out of it, and/or what you learned from it
--High school and college highlights
--Special girls you dated; might be nice to elaborate here
--The joys and sorrows of military service
--Some of the happiest times in your life
--Describe your relationship with parents, siblings and other family members

--The most important things you have learned from
family members and how it has influenced your life

If you are a young father, resolve to keep a journal or
notebook handy now, while your children are growing up so
that you can share your current perspective. Try to include
the aforementioned topics, but put special emphasis on your
thoughts and feelings at the time. You will be amazed at how
your perspective grows and matures over the years. Father's
Day would be an excellent time to start your journal (or even
to give to loved ones). Don't allow time restraints to keep
you from making random notes. Random notes are always
better than no notes. I promise you that your children and
grandchildren will cherish it for the rest of their lives. When
time permits and you decide to organize your notes into a
journal or binder to preserve for the future, here again, the
possibilities are endless. You can keep it simple or make it as
elaborate as you want.
   As for preservation of your information, if time is a
factor, the easiest and fastest way is to get it into a user
friendly, shareable format by incorporating the use of a
computer word program. You may wish to create chapters
like a book for each topic. As mentioned in a previous
chapter, storing them on the computer gives you the great
flexibility to add to them as things come to mind. (Just
remember to back up your files on a disc or flash drive in the
event of a computer problem.) When printing data off, punch
holes and add subject dividers to a binder. Should you decide
to add related photos, than you may want to opt for a
coordinating album. You can combine the journals with
photos in a formal or informal theme. If time is not a factor,

or you are a man who enjoys the creative element, there is a vast array of options for men who like to try their hand at adding an artistic touch to the pages. It is not for women only. Some men are very creative, and offer a unique perspective that we women may not have thought of. To add a little color and texture to your book, there are literally tons of masculine patterned papers and accents out there that are available to enhance your memories. For further information, please refer to the next chapter on "Preserving our heritage". You can also check out scrapbook sections of your local craft stores for additional ideas.

*****

Chapter Eleven

PRESERVING OUR HERITAGE

Choosing the Format

Some would say that with genealogy, our quest for information is never really complete. While that may be true to a certain extent, somewhere along the line, we must decide what method we would like to use to preserve the facts we have, as well as the memories. At some point you will want to transfer some, if not all, of your information to a format in which you can present/display it. This will be much more attractive, not to mention useful, than keeping it in a drawer or box. More importantly, you want to select the best and safest method to store all the data and memorabilia that you have spent time gathering. Some documents may be irreplaceable. Therefore, a safe and non-acidic storage system is a must.

Once again, it bears repeating: It can be as simple as recording known facts on charts or as detailed and elaborate as you would like it to be, up to and including keepsakes and memorabilia, from daily life to special events. It can also be a combination of data, charts, documents, your journaling of the memories, and/or photos. Make it whatever is the most meaningful to you.

While there are multiple ways of formatting the information we obtain, there are probably as many variations of each option as you can think of. Pick and choose what best meets the goal you have in mind. First you will need to decide what your goal is:

--Is it simply to record factual data like names, dates and places like a history book in a library?
--Is it to give your descendants the facts as well as to let them know something about these people they never had the opportunity to meet?
--Is it to put emphasis on the generational charts so they will know exactly whom they were descended from?
--Is it to let your descendants know family charts to tell them about who their second, third, fourth, etc. cousins may be?
--Is it to preserve memorabilia you have collected over the years?
--Is it to paint a better picture of life in times gone by with photos and human-interest stories?

The good news is you can do any or a combination of all of these. You can use several of the options to make your records into journals or albums that are truly unique. But let's make it clear, if you do not have the time or the desire to take it a step further with memory or scrapbooks, fact and note journals are perfectly fine. What really matters is preserving the information we have. You could simply print it out in the format you want and have copies made for relatives. Another option, giving it a little more of a professional appearance, is to consider self-publishing it through a site that prints it for a minimal fee, and on demand. One such site is: www.createspace.com

Memory books and scrapbooking formats are for those who have or are interested in developing their more creative side.

Consider these options or any combination of them:

The journal---What is a journal? There are mainly two types of journals. The first journal is something we enter data into, like a log, such as those used for a business. The second is more similar to a diary because it not only includes factual data, but our thoughts as well.

A journal can be in hardbound book form, a notebook, loose leaf in a three ring binder, a diary, or it can be stored on your computer and burned to any external drive, such as a CD, a DVD or a flash drive.

Some see it as a "text only" format that includes factual data about their lineage. It might also include the history of the surname. Others may see it in story form listing the facts about each family member along with pertinent details. You can also include stories on their likes and dislikes, personality traits, and even memories specific people have of them.

Memory books---The best way to describe a memory book is that they are similar to a scrapbook, but without the "scrap". They are usually, but not necessarily, more formal in format and design. They, like scrapbooks, make use of the **best-selected** memorabilia and photos, instead of all. They are sometimes designed with a theme in mind and will include photos, all significant data, and most importantly, the "journaling of memories", either in handwriting, computer fonts, or other forms. They may also incorporate actual documents or other memorabilia of their lives. Keepsakes too large for the book may be stored elsewhere, while a photo copy of it is, or can be, included in the book.

Scrapbooks---These will usually include all the elements of a memory book, but are usually much less formal and sometimes even whimsical. They are often made literally, with scraps of supplies, bits and pieces of memorabilia and often use the "torn paper" effect throughout.

Whatever method of storing and sharing you decide to do, always be sure it, as well as all other accents used, are photo safe, meaning acid and lignin free, to preserve them for generations to come. To keep memorabilia acid free, there is a spray available to neutralize acids. When using post bound, strap/hinge bound or loose leaf style binder albums, it is easy to add new pages in whatever order you wish as new information becomes available.

Photo albums---This is a traditional album normally used for photos only. You will need plenty of these, even if you are scrapbooking or doing memory books, to contain all the excess photos not used in them. It is a safer way to protect them rather than just tossing them into a box or a drawer.

A few words of caution; you may wish to avoid the use of a magnetic album. Modern ones may now be considered safe, but the older versions were notorious for the adhesives that were used, tending to adhere to the photos over a period of time. This made it virtually impossible to remove the photos without damaging or destroying them. They were not acid-free and caused the rapid deterioration of the paper, thus ruining the photos.

The best albums are those that are photo safe with acid and lignin free sleeves to slip photos in. There may or may not be room for any data to identify the photos. The nicer ones will include a small space for you to record vital information such as names, dates, places, etc. Many come with preprinted designs that are often color coordinated and sometimes, patterned backgrounds throughout. Although they are attractive, they normally don't allow you space to add much of your own creativity.

There are also **pre-done scrapbook albums** that are already coordinated for you with space to put your photos as well as space to "journal" (which, in this case, is what we call writing down your thoughts) along with dates, names, places and what the photo is about.

Then there are the **blank-inside scrapbooks** with wonderfully creative covers, but blank inside so that you can give your imagination free reign. These make-your-own kinds allow you to "start from scratch" to combine generational and family charts along with photos, text and even memorabilia. It doesn't have to be fancy if you don't want, but it can still be neatly organized and attractive.

Always use only photo safe pens, pencils or markers for identification, titling or journaling. Even if you decide to create a more elaborate memory album or scrapbook with some of the "select best" photos, you will still want a good album(s) to preserve and store the rest or duplicates for ease of viewing.

Themes for Heritage Albums

As you accumulate information you will come to realize that
not only is it impractical but also impossible to get everything
you have within one cover. It would eventually be so large
you couldn't lift it, even if you have the kind of album that is
expandable. Of course, you will choose the best photos to
include and **make copies**, rather than using the originals. It
is best to concentrate on one subject or theme at a time. This
means that you will be arranging your collected information
according to, and focusing on, a particular topic. Here are
some suggested themes or titles for heritage albums that
might include:

> ---"Our Heritage" or "Generations of Ancestors" (be sure
> to include photos of each, generational charts, and if
> possible, a map of the ancestral homeland in this one).
> ---"Christmas Past" or "Christmas through the Years"
> ---"Childhood Memories"
> ---"Weddings of Our Ancestors"
> ---"A Tribute To _____" (about an individual's life
> from birth to passing which may require more than one
> album).
> ---"Life's Path" (career)

The album itself---Select what will go best with the
theme you choose. The size will be determined by what you
want to put in it. For just a few photos and journaling, you
might prefer 8" x 8". That one, along with the 8 ½" x 11"

memory book, are excellent sizes for gifts. If, however, there is a lot you want to say or do, probably the most popular and best suited to your needs is the traditional 12" x 12". If you have a lot of good photos and memorabilia on any particular subject, you probably need to devote an entire album to that particular theme. You will always want to choose an album that has the protective plastic sleeves to protect your finished pages.

Next, you will need to decide if you want the entire album done in various shades and patterns of the same color, or if you want to incorporate many different colors and textures for adding contrast and interest. The front and back pages are normally single page layouts. I would suggest starting with a title page and ending with a tribute/dedication page (which defines its purpose) or even a personal note in a pocket for the person it is for, if it is to be a gift. Some prefer to incorporate this page right after the title page, instead of at the end. Throughout the rest of the album, you may want to consider doing two-page layouts that coordinate in theme and color.

Backgrounds---Your page backgrounds give you the opportunity to go simple, with preprinted solid or patterned papers, or to be very creative and combine any number of techniques you already know, or would like to try. Some of the best colors that work well for backgrounds or accents in "heritage themed" albums are the neutrals of black, gray, ivory, tan, chocolate browns, or dark jewel colors (such as navy/federal blue, forest/hunter green, deep red/wine), and of course, gold, silver and copper. The use of neutral or dark shades usually work best for showcasing older or antique photos, while ivory, tan and off-whites generally make great mats or accents. Metallic colors add an air of elegance.

Recommended Tools

Once you are ready to start your memory album, you may be at a loss as to what you really need to get the job done. Much depends not only on the type of memory album you have planned, but also the quantity of memory books you intend to work on. The wide array of possibilities available can be overwhelming when trying to decide what you really need.

For the genealogy portion of it, you will need, and probably already have, a file or binder in place for each family surname to keep near for quick and easy reference. It should include clear plastic protectors to slip documents into. It is usually best to make copies of these to use in your memory books. Include in here your generational and family charts. You may also want to purchase clear acrylic pockets to use to hold and preserve memorabilia.

For the memory book portion of it, if you already have advanced tools such as electronic die cutters for other projects, they can add much to your pages. However, be careful to preserve the dignity of vintage memorabilia with heritage-themed accents, vs. whimsical. You need not invest a lot of money in supplies to create beautifully themed heritage albums if you don't wish to, because you can make some fantastically creative albums with just a few basic supplies.

I would recommend starting with basic tools, especially if you don't plan to do many books or albums. Just like any specialty, new tools, especially those centered in technology, are always being invented. Shop around before purchasing to see what will best meet the needs of the goals you have in mind.

First, you'll need to choose an album in keeping with your theme and choose papers, both solid and patterned that will coordinate with it. There are certain tools that you will need for the job. I would recommend you invest in the following:

--A good paper cutter/trimmer is a must. You will use it for cropping photos and cutting papers to size.

--Decorative patterned scissors: Choose a simple, but elegant, or deckle-edged because they work especially well for heritage.

--Acid free markers, colored pencils and/or calligraphy pens: The colored pens are useful for outlining photos, labeling, journaling, free-hand drawing, and for emphasizing the patterns of patterned papers, etc.

--A few basic shaped punches: Punched shapes have both a positive and a negative image. The positive is, of course, the image you punched out. The negative is the piece of paper you punched it from. Trim it up with decorative scissors and you can eventually use it too. Larger ones work nicely to frame journaling or other accents. Some basic shapes you will find many uses for are circles, squares, hearts, and flowers. They will work for background, for borders, accents, lettering in titles, etc. Also, consider a corner punch, or at least a corner rounder to soften and add interest to photos or mats. --Rubber, foam or acrylic stamps along with acid-free ink pads: Any stamp that has a vintage theme, as well as basic shapes, including scrolls. You can create your own printed papers, backgrounds or mats with stamps. Create an antique or distressed look by inking the edges of pages, mats or torn papers. Use shapes as masks when stamping for a 3D effect. The possibilities are endless with even a limited number of stamps.

These are all tools that you don't use up (except for an occasional blade replacement). They are used repeatedly, and therefore are a good investment, particularly when you have many albums planned.

Elements to Use in Heritage Albums

After choosing the style of album we want to create, it is a good idea to take our page themes and the colors for our backgrounds from the photos or memorabilia we plan to work with.

When we think of heritage pages, we often think of reaching back in time before and after the turn of the last century for its motifs and accents. However, if we are making memory books for the coming generations, there will come a time when we will be gathering data and memorabilia, not just on those who came before us, but also on ourselves and our children so that we can include it. This means we will be researching and preserving data and memories from probably the forties through the eighties. We will want to use accents from those decades appropriate to the lifetime of those we are profiling. If you don't have actual keepsakes to use, libraries and the Internet can easily provide it. For a personal touch, interview your subjects while you still can and obtain a list of their favorite things, places and people in their lives to include in your books.

Consider beginning each generation with an overall page or two-page layout that includes both sets of parents, or the four grandparents, etc. Then elaborate on each of them in succeeding pages. The generational and/or family charts would be good to include here. Decide if and how you want to incorporate generational or family charts into the particular book you are working on. Factual data and documents can be combined with memory books, or you can do them in a special book of their own.

There are certain elements that are not only effective, but also work extremely well in setting the mood for a heritage/generational album. Obviously, it isn't practical to do them all—it is especially important to avoid clutter in heritage albums and think elegance, so choose the design elements and ideas you like best and get creative.

Suggestions to choose from include, but are not limited to the following:

Papers--Consider using one neutral background paper or monochromatic tones of the color scheme throughout the album. Using neutral or darker shades of a color, usually work best to showcase older or antique photos. Choose monochromatic tones in solids and coordinating classic prints. Classic floral prints (that are reminiscent of old wallpaper patterns) also add a nice touch. Ivory, tan or off whites usually work best for accenting, however, for a more elegant look, consider metallic or pearl-finished papers.

--More elegance might demand the look vellum can bring. Vellum adds an air of mystery and at the same time softens bolder colors. Vellum papers are rather transparent, come in white, prints and colors. They are wonderful for overlays and can be cut out to use over parts of a photo for emphasis in an oval or other special shape. The inner edges can be inked for emphasis to "frame" it. Vellum can even be embossed or written on. You can also use textured papers, pre-embossed or do-it-yourself. If you don't want to do the creative work, there are quite a variety of pre-printed nostalgic papers available.

--Another interesting accent is to split any 8 ½" x 11" sheets into panels for your background. This can also be done with vellum to overlay a colorful or patterned background paper. It softens/tone it down, so that it appears less busy.

--The cobblestone look on background papers adds a touch of a European influence to your layouts.

Mats and frames--The shape most frequently used to showcase old or antique photos seems to be the oval, although other ornate shapes can work just as well. Framing your titles or journaling in these shapes also adds a touch of class to your layouts.

--For a two-page layout, cut a large circle or oval for one side so that it can be used to frame the page and use the positive cut from it on the opposite side. This is not only a good way

to showcase photos, but is perfect for highlighting documents or telling your story either handwritten or via computer fonts.
--Pleat wide strips of paper into a circle to use as mats for photos. Vintage prints are perfect. Add accent by matting your photo first on a slightly wider solid color. You can also accent with a length of ribbon behind them to add an elegant touch.
--Fabric, especially authentic pieces from the past, make great backgrounds or mats, and you can include the story behind it.
--Torn edges of papers or mats give it the worn look. You can then ink or chalk the edges for an even more distressed look.
--Mats can also be made of woven, pleated or lattice-folded papers.
--They can be stenciled, embossed, or be creative, and use a combination of punches.
--Multiple mats in different sizes, shapes and colors can add contrast and elegance, giving it a layered effect.
--Mats can be solid or printed (and alternated), doubled or tripled.
--Real lace or paper doilies make excellent mats for photos, as well.
--Frames can be die-cut or made by using a corner punch on paper slightly larger than the photo to be used.

Corner punches—There are some that can be used to insert photos into so that adhesives aren't really necessary. It gives the appearance of a frame, and at the same time, adds interest with a little design. Consider using slotted or Iron Gate, as they work well for heritage.

--Cut corner designs can be used either on the actual photos or on the mats.

--Another option is to use old-fashioned photo splits for corners to insert the photos in. This also allows you to easily remove the photos, should anyone need additional copies. In this way, there is no damage from adhesives while trying to remove the photos.

 --Consider using rounded corner punches on photos, mats or frames for a softer look.

--The use of scallops in fan shapes for corners or borders also give the corners of photos a Victorian era look.

--Use triangle cut pieces of ribbon on the corners of photos or mats.

--Use punched images (such as small flowers) on some or all of the corners. For round or oval photos or frames, a small cluster of flowers at the top or bottom is an especially nice touch.

Pens, pencils, markers and fonts—Use "calligraphy" pens in black, brown, gold, silver or copper for titles or journaling. Calligraphy adds an "Old World" look to your pages.

For computer fonts, use a larger size fancy script font for titles or for the initial letter in the first word of a title or paragraph for emphasis.

Maps--Use a map of the ancestral area as a complete or partial background for pages or photo mats. Try to have pertinent places either highlighted or marked with an accent, either a star, or use a circle to simulate a magnifying glass. To showcase it, you might even cut the area out and mat it like a photo for emphasis.

*****

Adding character to our heritage pages is easy with the vast array of possibilities available to us. After choosing the type of album we want to create, the background, the color schemes, and the kinds of mats or frames we'd like for our photos, it's time to consider other accents that will emphasize our theme and add interest. Since we want to preserve the dignity of our heritage pages, not all accents would be appropriate, so choose your favorites.

Therefore, some possibilities that work extremely well for a heritage page are as follows:

Border choices—The use of borders gives the illusion of framing your page(s).
--Ribbon or lace panels
--Antique buttons (or rows of them)
--Stenciled or embossed patterns
--Woven strips of coordinating paper
--Die-cut or punched designs, especially in rope twist, floral, vine, elegant, lace, or lattice.

Corner choices— (Many are available to match the borders).
--Stamped   --Stenciled,

--Embossed   --Die-cut
--Punched   --Inked
--Try the look of paper doilies folded into fourths and cut for the look of lace
--Try wrapped in ribbon and/or accented with bows.

Design elements that go back decades—
--Decorative edge scissors, especially elegant designs and flourishes, or deckle edge, like those used in old photos.
--The use of ovals or other ornate shapes in backgrounds, mats, frames or embellishments take us back in time.

Buttons--An interesting way of using buttons on your pages, besides as borders, are as the center for flower accents. Actual ones from the era are even better, especially if they belonged to an ancestor.

Bookplates—Real ones are usually made of metal and add a vintage flair, but you can also use die-cut ones from cardstock. They not only "label" the photo, they create an air of prestige.

Nested motif accents--These can be simple or elaborate and add an air of old world charm.

Silhouettes—You may add an aura of mystery by making a silhouette out of black paper. It will create the look of a shadow.

Ribbon—Run a strip of ribbon down behind your framed photos, for elegance. Or use ribbon for frames or page borders. You can also place ribbon above some of the photos that are in frames in an inverted V-shape, as if they were wall hangings or hanging from a wire.

Titles—A title may be used anywhere on a page, not necessarily along the top; consider the bottom or down along the sides, or on top of a border. It can be lettering that is handwritten, stamped, stenciled, rubbed on, or stickers. The use of a calligraphy pen here for handwritten titles has a great impact, or to outline.

Journaling--Handwritten leaves a sample of your own personality. It can also be done inside of specific shapes or it may be written on vellum. The use of computer fonts makes the possibilities endless. Heritage style or antique script fonts not only make it elegant, but also add some old world charm. Be careful to choose those that are not too difficult to read. When using fancy fonts, avoid using all capitals or it will appear distorted.

Embellishments--This is a category that speaks volumes. In addition to the aforementioned elements of stamps, stickers, embossing, die-cuts or punches, here are others items to consider whether authentic or reproduced:
--Fabrics from that era
--Buttons from the time period
--Tags with titles, journaling or adornments on them

--Antiqued metal accents
--Specially adorned vellum envelopes or pockets for holding journaling or memorabilia.
--Clear window box cases are available for those 3D keepsakes you would like to include. However, they will take up additional space and add bulk to your album.
--Flowers
--Beads
--Glitter
--Wire
--Brads
--Eyelets
--Charms
--Acrylic gemstones
--Stickers, including 3D; however, some are not as suited to the heritage look, so be careful if you use those on heritage pages, as simpler is often better.

There are specific accents that are ideal to use for vintage photos. If you don't have the actual elements to use, you can always download images of them and copy from the Internet. Consider these:
--Antique or vintage frames
--Hinges
--Photo turns
--Antique keys
--Old trunks
--Victorian purses, high top shoes or heels
--Victorian fans, gloves, hats or other accessories
--Old clocks with Roman numeral faces, (or just the hands)

--Banners for names or titles
--Picket fences
--Scrolls
--Bookplates
--Fleur-de-lis accents
--Antique buttons
--An hourglass
--Windowpane with shutters
--Cathedral-style window
--Postcards from the time period (even if not original)
--Authentic memorabilia and keepsakes. Incorporate any cherished family memorabilia into your layouts, especially any postcards, notes or letters from the era, written to or from an ancestor.

Including Memorabilia

There are tons of other options for those who would like to incorporate a variety of memorabilia. In this case, it may be seen as the work of art that it can be, as you make it into a treasure to be handed down to others. First decide what you have that you want to preserve. Some of the things you want to consider including in any form of preservation are:

--Factual data, such as generational and family charts
--Legal documents, such as birth, marriage, death certificates, military records, immigration and census records, ancestral maps, and real estate deeds

--Personal documents, such as receipts, report cards or other school related data, cherished recipes

--Memorabilia, such as wedding, baby, baptismal or other religious events, travel souvenirs, obituaries and memorial cards

--Letters, notes, postcards, postage stamps of the era, as well as anything else that may contain handwriting samples of ancestors

--Newspaper clippings/articles (because they deteriorate quickly, be sure to copy them onto acid free paper)

--Memory journaling about our ancestors, as well as of our descendants

--And of course, photographs--Select the best and most unique and have copies made to use in your choice of album or method of preservation. Store the rest in acid free photo boxes or albums.

--Consider including maps of the areas that ancestors came from.

Once you know what you have to work with, you'll need to decide what you want to combine under one cover. Factual data and legal documents, being more formal, work well together in the same journal or album. Acid free page protectors should always be used to keep all legal documents clean. This organizes all the factual data neatly and in a format that is easy to follow. Actually, there really isn't any reason why you can't have it both ways. Another way to include them is to create page pockets in which to insert them.

This would leave the fun stuff to be combined in any format you wish. It just takes a little organizing in the beginning and assembling the things you will need. That doesn't mean you can't include some of the things you've put into the factual journal. In fact, that could be important when telling a story in words or pictures in your albums or scrapbooks. Some prefer to use the word "memory" book rather than "scrapbook". As previously stated, the word 'scrapbook' seems to conjure up visions of bits and pieces of unrelated materials tossed into a binder of sorts. Way back at the turn of the century that is exactly what they were, things salvaged from the past. Many of today's scrapbooks are very reminiscent of that with their shabby chic and "patchwork quilt" design. However, gaining in popularity and my personal favorite is the newer trend of making them a little more formal if not elegant, and artsy. Many can become real works of art in their design and at the same time allow you the opportunity to be creative no matter what your gender.

Preserving Family Secrets

Without a doubt, there will be times that you come across information that may be sensitive to some people. There are several ways to deal with this, and preserve it, without making it available to anyone who may view a family journal/memory book.

In any kind of journal log, memory book, or scrapbook, you can use "hidden journaling". What is hidden journaling? It is the keeping of pertinent information in such a way that it is not readily noticeable or accessible, but still available to be a part of our history. No matter what kind of book format you use, there are ways to secretly preserve the information. Here are some ideas:

---Even if you are only doing a journal format, you will have placed your charts into clear acid free protective sleeves. You simply tuck the information in question down behind that person's page or generational chart. It is there for those who know to access it, but away from any eyes that may just be browsing. What a treasure it will be for descendants to eventually find little known facts or secrets along with the feelings, in their journals and memory books.

---It can be as simple as writing on the back of top loading pages or photos that are not permanently glued down. To do this with the photos, use either the old-fashioned corner photo splits, or mats that have punched corners for inserting the photos. In this way you can lift them out as needed.

---Another option is to write or type the information on separate acid free cardstock and tuck it in between front and back facing pages within your page protector.

---Make lift up accents that hide the journaling text and/or hidden photos. This makes them rather inaccessible to the untrained eye, and being in a page protector offers added security.

---Make a "photo size" pocket and mat your photo on it, then tuck the story down in. They'll assume it's just a mat.

---Create a mini booklet, tri-fold, or accordion style booklet and hide behind any another page element.

---Create a puzzle. Journal on colorful cardstock and cut it into pieces. Place in a shaker box made for memory book keepsakes. They will think it is only colored paper. (Placing it in an envelope would work too.)

---Or place it in a sealed envelope in a specially made "pocket page" with the "after date" to open. Pocket pages are also great for holding keepsakes.

---How about a time capsule? This is for things you don't necessarily want known today, but are not opposed to in the future. You can do it like a pocket in fabric or cardstock. Stitch it up with a basting stitch and attach a tag with the date it can be opened. Another option is to use a zipper at the top if you want, with the tag attached to the zipper pull.

*****

Alternatively, if you have someone who absolutely does not want certain facts be made known in their lifetime, consider recording any such information, placing it in a sealed envelope and adding it to your safety deposit box (or giving to the attorney). In this way, anything that is important enough for them to know can eventually be added to the family history without being lost forever. You may wish to ask the person who wants their secret kept until after their passing, if they would like to write it themselves to give their perspective on the situation.

Hidden journaling does not have to be about secrets or information on difficult topics. You might wish to include sentimental thoughts, feelings, what you learned from your mistakes, how life's lessons have affected the person you have become, predictions for a child's future, future wedding day wishes, letters written to loved ones upon your passing, etc. Use your imagination.

Tools for Advanced Memory Books

Suppose you have advanced to the point that you want it all. This section is for those who would like to take preservation to the next level. There are ways to do so while keeping it neatly organized and without it looking cluttered.

You might consider doing it in two formats. Factual data and legal documents, being more formal, work well together in the same binder, journal or album. It is the perfect format for the bulk of your historical data and would also be a nice place to include maps of the ancestral homeland.

Remember, it may be necessary to include some of these basic facts in your memory albums or your scrapbooks. You will then devote the bulk of your memory albums/scrapbooks to photos, and the journaling of your thoughts and memories of the places and people in the photos. Finally, add to it any memorabilia you have acquired.

If you want it fast, there are tons of themed albums you can buy and just add photos and journaling, as mentioned in and earlier section. There are also a variety of ready-made supplies available, such as previously formatted albums, paper, stickers, frames, mats and embellishments that you can purchase.

However, if you love art and the opportunity to be creative, you can make it a do-it-yourself project and a real treasure of your creativity that your loved ones will enjoy for years to come. Preprinted materials don't always allow you the opportunity to be as creative as you might like. Some prefer starting from scratch, by determining the kind of books they want to create, the theme, choosing the album, coordinating patterned and solid color papers. Again, since possibilities are endless, it is great stimulation for your imagination. Making some of your own embellishments with die cuts, ribbon, rubber stamps, inks, etc. is also a very creative outlet.

The more elaborate, the more time and money you could have invested in it. Therefore, I would recommend that you invest in tools that you will use repeatedly. In that case, you will have them to use for a variety of projects. However, it is entirely possible to make beautiful albums with just a few basic tools and supplies.

Once the materials have been assembled, it is "inspiration" time. Borrow ideas from books, magazines, and things around you. Have a mental picture of what you'd like the finished product to look like and the sentiments you want to convey. Make a list of the things you would like to include so you don't forget anything. You can decide later where you want to place them. Make an additional list of the things you want to say including both facts and thoughts on the subject that you can journal (write) about.

With that said, for those who would like to express a little more creativity and also like more of a challenge, here are some ideas you may want to try. You can actually make your books a work of art. While basic supplies are sufficient to make some fabulous memory books, there are other options that could be a wise investment, particularly if you plan to make many memory books. They work whether you are making multiple books filled with historical data, generational and family data, photos or other memorabilia.

You could invest in a good **cutting system** that will cut shapes for frames and mats or even crop photos. It can be a lever, feed through, or rapidly becoming the most popular method, are the electronic cutting system machines. There are many on the market and it is pretty much a matter of preference, and what your ultimate goals are. Just be sure to read the packaging for what is included, and what the specifications are to help you decide. There are also a variety of circle and other shape cutters, both electronic and manual, and some even as simple as templates. Again, you can cut actual photos with them or they are useful as frames, mats, or blocks for journaling or for framing embellishments. They are, however, a good investment only if usage justifies the price.

While some people consider **rubber stamps** a basic need, the truth is, you don't need a lot of them unless you choose to. They are no longer just rubber mounted on wood. In addition to wood, they now come in other forms such as foam and the ever-popular acrylic. Acrylics have the distinct advantage of being see-thru, since they cling, which makes them terrific for accuracy in placement. Stamps come in about any design you can imagine, including alphabet fonts, as well as words and phrases that make doing titles easy.

As for **embellishments**, if you can imagine it, you can either buy it or make it. There are stickers, even 3-D ones in themed designs. Fabrics, silk flowers, ribbon, buttons, wire, brads, eyelets, paper doilies and metal accents, all add that extra emphasis to advanced pages. Just be careful not to overdo for heritage albums, as you want to avoid the cluttered look, since it will detract from your focal points. It is best to select two or three types of accents to use throughout a two page spread and then use in repetition. Repetition is eye appealing and adds interest. You will want these pages to be dignified, yet personal.

If you enjoy creativity, there are some advanced **techniques** you may want to try.

Embossing can be done with texture plates on your papers for background or embellishing frames or mats. It can also be done with pressure either with a stylus or machine. You can then elect to chalk or ink the embossed images.

Chalking or inking can be done not only to embossed images, but also to edges for a distressed look. These are ideal for the heritage look. Be sure that all chalks and inks used are specially formulated for archiving, so that they are safe and acid free.

Rub-ons—stickers, available in images, words or phrases.

Note to the Men

If time is a factor, preserve what you have acquired, written or recorded entirely in journal form for now. You can always expand on it later and turn it into an album. However, if you are a man who enjoys the creative element, there is a vast array of options for men who like to try their hand at adding an artistic touch to the pages. It is not for women only, many men are actually quite good at it, and offer a unique perspective that we as women, may not have thought about.

To add a little color and texture to your books, there are literally tons of masculine patterned papers and accents available to enhance your memories.

Some men enjoy designing their own history books, and creating a heritage album to leave for their children. It is certainly a legacy your children will cherish for a lifetime.

*****

Chapter Twelve

PHOTOS

Preserving Old Photographs

Are you lucky enough to have inherited some old black and white photos? Chances are that they are in old albums and are a part of your very history. If this is the case, you may have observed some damage to them due to their deterioration over the years. Many old albums are of black construction paper sandwiched between heavy black cardboard covers and held together by string. The photos themselves may be held in place by glued photo corners.

These images probably date from about 1918 through the 1930's. It is important to their preservation that you get them out of that environment and into an acid and lignin free system. Any damage is likely due to the fact that the papers and glue were not acid free and in some cases not color fast, so that if they became wet or even damp, the color can run onto the photos. Where they were stored will also affect the rate at which they deteriorate because of light and temperature changes.

In years gone by, people were largely unconcerned with photo safety, as the acidic damage to photos was not yet known. Over time, the acid causes the photos to become brittle and the adhesive in the glue seeps into the images, staining them. Once color prints came into popularity in the 60's, it became apparent that colors would shift and fade. Something had to be done to preserve these precious mementoes. Extreme care must be used when transferring these old photos to another system. Whenever possible, they should be arranged in the particular order that they were in. This is for the specific reason of not losing any family history that the person who put it together was trying to preserve. Be sure that you save any captions associated with the photos. They may be removed more easily, if they are in photo corner pockets. If they are glued to the pages, you may try to gently lift them by very slowly running dental floss down behind them. (Tie the two ends of it to metal key rings to keep it from cutting into the fingers). If it appears that they may tear, scan either the photos or the entire pages instead. (Then you can store the originals in an acid free cloth or box).

It might be a good idea to invest in an inexpensive scanner of your own and copy each page. You can then print out the images on a photo printer using acid free photo paper. Be sure to save any captions that go with them. Don't forget to add your own thoughts to the new album, for a multigenerational perspective. Also, be sure to check the backs of the originals for pertinent information before securing in another storage system.

Meanwhile, remember that those scanned images are perfect for sharing with other interested family members, either by emailing or printing off to share.

Postmortem Photography

When you have been researching family history for any length of time, you have no doubt come across old photographs of deceased family members.

A little background—according to Internet resources, photography began in 1839 in France. It was considered to be an expensive luxury and thus the making of a portrait became a memorable occasion for Victorian Americans. Due to the expense involved, some folks never had the opportunity to take advantage of it as a way of preserving their heritage. In many instances, postmortem photos were the only photos of the deceased ever taken. Therefore, making memorial photography an extra special memento of a life lost. In photography's early years, death was still widely considered an important and natural part of everyday life. People took photographs of their deceased loved ones with a reverence that is rarely understood today. Such photos were considered to be a normal part of their culture and allowed families a tangible visual object that allowed continued closeness to those loved ones.

Postmortem photography also reflects more general social circumstances. Especially with the high infant mortality rates of bygone times, photos of their deceased children became precious memories to grieving parents. I am able to relate to this first hand, as I was lucky enough to obtain a rare and the "only" photo ever taken of my mother's sister, Irene, who passed away in 1928 at the age of 13 months. What a beautiful baby she was and we would never have known that, if they had not gotten a photographer to take a picture of her even though they were grieving.

Sometimes, even the elderly never had the opportunity to be photographed. The family calling in the photographer was their final chance to be remembered as they were in this world. The custom was for the deceased to be laid out sometimes at a funeral parlor, but more often at home, and the photographer would visit to pay his last respects and take that final photograph. It was popular to place the deceased on a sofa or bed at home, perhaps elevated by a pillow, and then posed comfortably, to give the appearance of sleep. Frequently, props were added to the setting, such as a cross, rosary, a toy or special keepsake, and of course, plenty of flowers to mask any odor of decomposition.

The photographs were then kept as a remembrance and sent to relatives that could not make the long hard trip to attend the funeral. As home photography became practical and affordable, postmortem photographs lost favor and went out of style. In our modern culture it is usually considered to be morbid or in bad taste and is not allowed by some funeral homes. It is basically now used primarily for forensics.

Attempting to place an old postmortem photo into its correct time period does not have to be a tedious process. If you already know the time period in which the subject lived, great. If not, determine the type of photograph that it is. Time frames for the various photographic processes can be found in books or online and are a tremendous help for establishing a timeline.

The Importance of All Photos

Photographs are a part of history, a moment captured in time and a pictorial history of people, places, and things. In most cases, they cannot be retaken. It could be that the time has passed, the subject(s) will never be that age again, or the places no longer look the same, because all things change in some way. Therefore, the history in photographs is irreplaceable.

Though they may not matter to you, they may be the only link someone has someday to their family history. If you personally do not want them, please do not destroy them. Consider giving these unwanted photos to other persons who will someday want or need them. It could be a relative; or if you don't know who that would be, consider donating them to a local genealogy or historical society. Some libraries may even accept them. Someday, someone may be able to identify the places or subjects. Therefore, it would be a community service to allow others to enjoy them. There are also places online that may buy your old photographs, especially vintage ones.

Before donating, just be sure to check the backs of old photographs for any pertinent information. Many of us have inherited photos that were not marked; therefore, we can't identify the subjects in them. Not much can be done except for asking the elders in the family if they can give us a clue. Let it be a lesson to us to be sure to label (title) and date ours so that our families will not face the same problem. (In our digital age, many cameras now include the date taken.)

It may also be that those that the photographs would have mattered to, have already passed and they mean little to those left behind. Perhaps you don't know or just plain don't remember who someone is in the photo. The same rules for donating apply.

Sometimes people discard photos, old or not, because a relationship ends. At that time, they may not feel like they will ever want to look at them again, and sometimes there is even a sense of loss, similar to when there is a death in the family. They may find them too painful to look at. Moreover, if it was a bitter parting, one or the other of the involved party's first reaction is to destroy the photos, hence destroying the bad memories. But it doesn't work that way. It is at that time in our history that we learned some very important lessons.

Traditionally, photos were most often taken on special occasions, and to preserve holiday memories. However, scrapbooking has made a new trend popular; to capture everyday moments as a snapshot in time. With the digital age of cameras and smart phones, it is easier than ever. But it is equally important as we organize them and upload them to our computers or external drives, that we be sure we take the time to label the pictures with names and places. Again, dates automatically show up on most of today's technology.

You may have noticed that sizes of photos have changed over the years with both the type of camera used and the film speed. You can also figure the approximate timeframe of unmarked photos by the style of the finished product. Each decade had its trends. Remember the black and white with deckled edges in booklet albums of the 50's? In the 70's they were just about square with a mini duplicate version and the colors did not always set well. Many now have a yellow cast from being stored in early magnetic albums. Of course, the trend now is the ever popular 4" x 6" as evidenced by the many ready-made albums available in that size.

Note to photo industry manufacturers—Many of us still have the older sizes of pictures that we want and need safe photo storage and albums for. It would be nice if these were specifically designed to accommodate those older sizes. When enough of us request them, they may begin to see the need.

*****

Chapter Thirteen

LEAVING A LEGACY

Legacy Writing

Legacy writing is another unique part of our genealogy that may never have occurred to us to record. It also differs somewhat from our memoirs, because it isn't just another autobiography. With legacy writing, we concentrate on our thoughts and feelings, recording them for our descendants. In this way, they have an opportunity to know us, without ever having met us. It does not deal so much with lineage and fact as it does with character and values.

In the beginning, not many of us thought about the importance of writing down our thoughts about the different milestones in our life. There have been times when we knew we were obviously opening a new chapter in our lives, and we probably had much to say about it at the time, but never took the time to write it down. Ironically though, our descendants will no doubt face some of those same challenges in their lives. How helpful would it be to let them know how we dealt with it and how the results changed us? Among the many scenarios, this could have to do with positives such as meeting and marrying the person of our dreams, receiving an inheritance you did not expect, meeting long lost family, and the joy of adding a new infant or child to the family. Let us not forget to make note of how good life has been to us, what made us happy, our hopes and dreams, achieving a particular goal or landing that dream career, our courage and convictions and above all, our faith in a higher power.

It is equally as important to record the negative times in our lives. With legacy writing, however, our descendants will probably learn the most from how we handled the adversity we faced, examples being: a divorce, the loss of a child, the passing of any loved one, especially those younger than ourselves. Don't forget to write about the painful moments such as emotional or physical abuse suffered. Not only will it help them to understand us, our writing of it alone can be therapeutic in and of itself.

Sometimes when looking through old city directories or even census records, we find out something we might refer to as one's "residential" history. This often poses more questions than it answers. What prompted them to move: loss of job, a divorce, a foreclosure, or to be near other family members? Was it a move across town or across the country, or was it finally reaching the American dream of obtaining the first home of their own? Wouldn't it be wonderful to know what was going on in their lives and in their minds at that time? In any case, these events planned or otherwise, very often opened new chapters in their lives.

In the following segment are some random topics in no particular order, to help you to start thinking about what you would like people to know or learn from your life. Write about what values you want to pass on, and how important these values are to you. Stories of our lives are gifts to be given to others that will be cherished forever. In other words, it is sharing with them our personalities, experiences and the wisdom that we acquired throughout our lifetime.

Questions for Legacy Writing

Some of these topics may not appear to be quite as important to document in the quest to preserve our heritage. However, I feel that they are just as important, because they tell our descendants who we really were. They are also the foundations for the human-interest stories that will be handed down from one generation to another. (These questions could also be asked of those we interview.) Since some of them are very personal, include or exclude, as you feel comfortable and/or include your own.

Here are just a few questions to contemplate when thinking of writing your own memoirs:

--Who was your favorite childhood playmate?

--What did you want to do with your life when you were only five years old? Fifteen? Twenty-five?

--What did you get in trouble for as a child?

--As a teenager, what incident with your parents angered you most?

--Do you remember your wildest party?

--With whom did you share your first kiss?

--What was your most profound moment in romantic love?

--How did you lose your virginity?

--What was your most memorable moment of family love?

--Have you ever felt like a hero?

--Name a time you were on top of the world.

--What did you do with your first big paycheck?

--What was your greatest success in your career?

--What do you feel was the biggest sacrifice you ever made?

--Name a time you fell flat on your face.

--Have you ever stolen anything?

--What is one habit you have that no one knows about?

--What were the most embarrassing things that have ever happened to you?

--What do you consider to be the dumbest things you ever did and what did you learn from them?

--Excluding comedy, what are the funniest things that you have ever witnessed over the years?

--What are you most proud of accomplishing in life?

--Have you ever had a supernatural or unexplained experience or know someone who did?

--You've heard the expression, "Regrets—I have had a few". If you could go back and make a change, what would it be?

While a cover page is not necessary to your legacy writing, it will add emphasis to the highlights of your memoirs or memories. The following is just a sample of a "cover page" to use in your legacy writing. Adapt it any way you wish that is most meaningful to you.

*****

Personal Legacy Letter of _____

Today's Date _____
*My current age*_____

Dear _____,

I am writing to share the personal legacy of my life. My intention is to let you know my thoughts and feelings about the life I have lived, to honor the relationships that have enriched my life, and to express my **gratitud**e *for*
_____.

Reflections on my values and life lessons:
What I have valued most in my life is . . .
My life experience has taught me . . .

My special memories and cherished moments:
Some of the most special memories I have are of . . .
I especially cherish the moments when...

Reflections on my spiritual beliefs:
I believe . . .
What gave me the most strength through
 difficult times was . . .

Expressions of any regrets and forgiveness:
If I could go back and change anything,
it would be...

I also regret the time when . . .
I forgive . . .
I ask your forgiveness for. . .

Future hopes and wishes:
My hopes for all of you include . . .
I ask that you . . . (any special requests) . . .
Expressions of gratitude and love:
I am most grateful for...
What I love about each of you is...

Last thoughts and blessings:
If I were saying "good-bye" to you today for the last
time, I would want you to know . . .
May your lives be blessed with . . .

Your handwritten
Signature *... ... ...*

Creating a Time Capsule
for Our Descendants

In a previous chapter, it was suggested that a note be left for
those who come after us. This would ttell them anything that
they may have needed to know or that we wanted them to
know, including how much they meant to us. What if we
were to take it one step further and give them a bigger
glimpse into our lives, just as we received when we
researched the lives of our ancestors? Imagine the impact it

could have in helping them to understand who and what we stood for and the circumstances we lived through.

A time capsule may be anything you want it to be. It can consist of only a document or a letter or it can be included in a container of items that will be sealed and put into safe keeping to be opened at a specified time, anywhere from 50 to 100 years from now. That could span four or five generations.

The time capsule container itself---as for the actual storage container, heavy gauge polyurethane or composite is longest lasting, but you must be sure it is both air and water-tight. There are professionally manufactured time capsules available on line in assorted sizes to best preserve your articles. The container can be handed from generation to generation or buried with explicit instructions as to where and when it is to be opened.

What might we include in a time capsule? It will, of course, be determined by the size of the container being used. Any of these items would be good choices to consider:

--Personal notes or letters, describing your hopes and dreams for them
--Photos—(Be sure that your photos are stored in acid free, photo safe sleeves for preservation.)
--Diary--that perhaps describes what life was like for you
--Books that had special meaning to you
--Heirloom jewelry
--Stamps
--Coins
--Recipes

--Badges

--Small bottle of wine

--Political/election memorabilia

--Magazines or catalogs

--Auto brochures of the time

--Business cards

--Phone book

--TV guide

--Legal documents

--Newspapers or articles—So that they may read about geographical events, current entertainment, including hit music and movies, weather stories, local and social events, weddings and obituaries, sports of the time, grocery ads, average prices of housing, real estate, autos, clothing, and flyers for our "modern day" technology. (All newspaper articles should be photo copied onto acid free cardstock to minimize deterioration. If using actual magazines and newspapers, there are archival sprays that you can purchase to neutralize acids and render them safe.)

--Consider also including some fun items to bring a smile to their faces, like a frilly little nightie. You get the idea. (But keep it clean, please.)

--Do NOT, however, use actual technology or media such as tapes, CD's etc. as this technology won't exist by then to utilize them.

No matter how you choose to do it, remember that it is part of a legacy that your heirs will cherish. It will be just like discovering a "treasure chest", buried or not, and one of the best legacies we can leave for the generations to come.

Chapter Fourteen

OUR VALUES & TRADITIONS

The entirety of this chapter might very well be incorporated into your legacy writing, because it is so closely related to what we want our descendants to know and inherit from us.

"What Will Matter"

For some time now, there has been a certain poem circulating on the Internet, and it was recently brought to my attention again, prompting me to share it for those who do not have computer access. It is not one of those emails that circulate purely for entertainment. This one was serious enough as to have a profound impact on those who put it together in this format in order to share it. The original author is Michael Josephson. His poem is both beautiful and meaningful. It is even much more powerful if you listen to the song "You'll Never Walk Alone" (original by Rogers & Hammerstein), as you read and contemplate it. You can always download the song from www.youtube.com.

*****

*****

"What Will Matter"

"Ready or not,

someday it will all come to an end.

There will be no more sunrises, no minutes, hours or days.

All the things you collected, whether treasured or forgotten,

will pass to someone else.

Your wealth, fame and temporal power

will shrivel to irrelevance.

It will not matter, what you owned or what you were owed.

Your grudges, resentments, frustrations and jealousies

will all disappear.

So, too, your hopes, ambitions, plans

and to-do lists will expire.

The wins and losses that once seemed

so important will fade away.

It won't matter where you came from or

on what side of the tracks you lived at the end.

It won't matter whether you

were beautiful or brilliant.

Even your gender and skin color

will be irrelevant.

So what will matter? How will
the value of your days be measured?
What will matter is not what you bought,
but what you built;
Not what you got, but what you gave.
What will matter is not your success,
but your significance.
What will matter is not what you learned,
but what you taught.
What will matter is every act of courage,
compassion, integrity or sacrifice,
that enriched, empowered or encouraged
others to emulate your example.
What will matter is not your competence,
but your character.
What will matter is not
how many people you knew,
but how many will feel a lasting loss
when you're gone.

What will matter are not your memories,

but the memories that live

in those who loved you.

What will matter is how long

you will be remembered,

by whom and for what.

Living a life that matters

doesn't happen by accident.

It's not a matter of circumstance,

but of choice.

Choose to live a life that matters".

*****

Perhaps you wonder what this poem has to do with our quest to uncover our heritage. It is in the line that says it is "not your memories, but the memories that will live in those who loved you", whether it is about our ancestors or our descendants.

*****

Counting Our Blessings &
Sharing Our Traditions

Harvest time, a time of year when we enjoy the fruits of our labor, also means we do some serious contemplating of what we have to be thankful for. With the beautiful colors of fall, come the first hints of the crisp cool air that ushers in the beginnings of the winter to come. It is the time of the year when nature goes to sleep so that it can renew itself yet again. For those who have suffered past losses at this time of year, it may be another reminder of the hard times they have experienced in their lives. For others, it can be the mark of new beginnings. Whatever the case may be, it's the time of year when we are reminded to appreciate what we have, as there is always someone who has less.

As we are researching our family history, we might discover how truly little our ancestors made do with. Material things meant little to them. Most of them had very little in resources, partly due to the Great Depression, so they directed their energies into taking care of their families as best they could and building their relationships. Their wealth was the vast array of family and friends that surrounded them. They had a deep sense of values as to what really mattered in this life. A large majority were first generation immigrant families who tried to pass on their native language and customs to their children, so that their heritage would not be forgotten.

You may well uncover evidence of this as you research, but you may have to rely largely on relatives for the human-interest stories. However, you can research real estate records to find out about their land holdings. These records will probably tell you how much they owned, its location and perhaps the value of it at that time. By today's standards, they had very little to work with and their opportunities were limited.

For men, unless you were in the minority of professionals, options were pretty much limited to mining and farming, and especially so, if you were an immigrant. However, they were thankful to have jobs to take care of their families. The vast majority of women did not work outside the home. Those that did were normally limited to teaching, nursing or perhaps helping a husband to run a business, such as a mercantile. Yet they did not see it as anything but a blessing. They did what they had to do and accepted it as their role in life. Most did not know the pressures of not being able to be at home with their children. In this sense they were lucky to be able to tend to their families, without the pressures of an outside job. Because of distance and prices, they didn't often have access to store bought, so necessity made it routine to make their own foods, clothing, household items, etc. Thus, customs and traditions were handed down from one generation to the other.

Maybe this is why some find the Amish so fascinating. They have managed to preserve that past, yet prosper in today's society. There is a pride in the simplistic lifestyle that some find they have difficulty in duplicating.

*****

It is absolutely important to count our blessings all year, but holiday time is the perfect time to share and pass down our traditions. Traditions bring us closer as a family and fill our hearts with the warmth of the memories we cherish. They remind us of the blessings we have shared and at the same time connect us with people, places and even objects we cherish. We have all practiced certain traditions of our ancestors over the years. These may be religious, social, secular or so on. Whether or not we choose to practice them is our choice. However, it is essential that we record them anyway.

Whatever your faith, traditions are important to all of us. They give us a sense of where we have come from and where we are going. These are also tremendous clues for our descendants to know where to look for glimpses into our lives. Be sure to make note of how the tradition got started and by whom, if known. Traditions may change over the years or they may be modified and new ones can be added. The important thing is that we make it meaningful. It is important that we write down what the family's traditions were, even if we don't currently practice them.

Have you participated in any of these traditions? Or maybe you'd like to start some with your children and grandchildren. Trying to do them all would be impossible and exhausting. Better to choose a few of the most meaningful ones to you. However you celebrate the seasons of life, these are a few traditions you may already practice, or add, for a memorable holiday season:

--Start the season out by watching a holiday movie together as a family.

--Keep an Advent calendar or its equivalent, depending on your faith, and do something special each day.

--Light an Advent wreath or its equivalent.

--Read a special story or scriptural passage together.

--Consider a family gift exchange in large families to lighten the financial burden.

--For light-hearted fun, include a gag gift (in good taste, please) to be passed around from year to year.

--Start any holiday shopping on Thanksgiving weekend or before, to spread out expenses.

--Instead of spending a lot of money on gifts, limit it, and spend the rest on adopting a family or giving to a food pantry.

--Send holiday greetings and/or care packages to our troops.

--Participate in an angel tree project.

--Attend or participate in holiday bazaars.

--Handcraft some ornaments or other décor together.

--Choose and/or decorate the perfect tree together.

--Designate a specific ornament on the tree for each family member.

--Bake and decorate cookies with someone special.

--Have and share specific special recipes you make for this season of the year; examples: spiced cider, pumpkin rolls, nut rolls, fudge, fruitcake, eggnog, etc.

--Go out as a family and take a tour of the lights and decorations.

--Go caroling, and don't forget to include the hospitals and nursing homes.

--Volunteer to work or serve meals in a food kitchen.

--Attend area church or school, holiday programs or perhaps a live Nativity Scene.

--Attend Christmas Eve or Day services or Midnight Mass.

--Spend the holidays "at Grandma's house" or better yet, change the tradition and have Grandma come to your house.

In addition to previously mentioned widely practiced traditions, here are some additional ones you may find heartwarming to start.

--Practice random acts of kindness, for you know not, who is in severe need at that particular moment. It may inspire others to want to pass it on.

--Do something nice for someone disabled or shut-in.

--Bring Christmas to a family in need by helping meet their needs, be it with food, transportation, clothing, toys for the children, or help with the heat bill. Get your family involved.

--Every year or perhaps more often, allow your children to select a toy of their own that is still in good condition to give to a child they may even know, who may not have much.

--Take the kids or grandkids to see Santa or volunteer to take kids when their parents or guardians cannot.

--Be Santa for someone whom you know doesn't have family nearby.

--Since we can all be Santa to someone, dress in a Santa suit and add some holiday cheer where you know it is most needed. Santa could even pass out candy canes.

--Consider gift certificates for goods or services like car washes, house cleaning, yard work, etc. for the elderly. This is especially important to them when they don't have family close by to help with difficult tasks. They need not be formal or professional certificates, but given by you from the heart.

--Invite elderly friends for an occasional meal, be it at your home or lunch out. Not only will they get a good meal, most meaningful to them, will be the opportunity to have great company.

--If you know someone who is going through an especially difficult time during the holiday season due to loss or serious illness, arrange for family, friends or neighbors to take turns providing a "heat up" or carry in a homemade or even a fast food meal for the family.

--Offer to sit with home confined individuals for a couple of hours to give the caregivers a break.

--Become a philanthropist, (one who donates time or money, often anonymously, for the good of mankind) even if it's only on a small scale.

--If you are one of those whom this time of year is especially painful for due to grieving the loss of a loved one, then there is no better remedy for sorrow then to become involved in meeting the needs of others to honor the memory of our loved ones.

There are, of course, many other ideas you may already do. Just be sure to record them. No matter what you do to bring a smile to someone else's face, it will end up warming your heart in a way that nothing else can. It's another way of giving back the blessings we have.

As we count our blessings, the importance of recording all the things and people we are grateful for should become clearer. It will be part of the legacy we leave for our descendants. Spending time with family and friends during the holiday season affords us the perfect opportunity to reflect with them not only on the events of this past year, but also those memories of bygone years when we were all together. It gives us the perfect opportunity at get-togethers to seek information from family members on ancestor's names, dates and other pertinent information. You'll be surprised how it brings the present into perspective and points us in the right direction for the future. At the very least, it will spark some interesting discussions at family gatherings.

The Gift of Parents

Some of us have been blessed to have had parents that taught us right from wrong, whether it was the popular thing to do or not. Growing up, there are sure to have been times when we were less than loveable. But many parents consider it their job and their calling to love their children unconditionally. That doesn't mean they condone any negative behavior, only that they forgive and love us anyway. If you are a parent, you now realize what your parents went through to raise you to be a responsible caring person.

Of course, not every mother/father and child relationship is without problems. Sometimes a parent can fall short of the kind of parent they should or want to be. Even then their children are learning from them. Sometimes they learn that they don't want to repeat the mistakes of their parents. Most of the time, parents are doing the best they can with the resources they have and what they themselves were taught. When children are grown and gone they will come to realize this and appreciate us for it. They will then understand the reasons we made some of the choices we made.

There are a few other kinds of moms and dads that deserve our thanks as well:

The "biological" parent who, out of love for their child, gives up their parental rights because they want their child to have a home and things they cannot give them. Their motives were unselfish even though their heart may have been broken. Someday, they will know they did the right thing.

The "adoptive" parent, who willingly gives up their time to share all their resources for the good of a child they often don't know, yet they are knowingly making a lifetime commitment.

The "foster" parent, who is usually ready at a moment's notice to take care of a child in need for as long as it takes. They do this, all the while, knowing they will ultimately have to give that child up.

The "stepparent", who not only takes another man's or woman's child into their home, but also takes them into their heart. In this way, they now have two moms and/or two dads to love and care for them, thus creating a healthy blended family so that the child will feel secure.

Then there is the "mom or dad-in-law". Although
mothers-in-law (and sometimes fathers-in-law) have gotten a
bad rap over the years, many love the spouses of their
children as their own and that love and respect is often
mutual. What a beautiful blessing to all concerned.

And my favorite, the "grand-mom/or dad"--until you
hear those words, "Good Grandma!" you don't fully realize
or understand the meaning of the word as it relates to the
circle of life.

For those who are lucky enough to have either of your
parents still living, consider writing a note in a card or giving
them a letter detailing the special memories they have given
you. I can assure you that they will feel it is one of the best
presents they have ever received. Chances are great that they
will save it, and it will be something that they will treasure
for the rest of their lives. Eventually, it will be added to your
journal/keepsakes. More importantly, you will have the
satisfaction of knowing you did not wait too long to let them
know they were appreciated. Father's Day, Mother's Day or
even their birthdays may seem like the ideal time, but it is a
safe bet that it will be appreciated on a "just because" kind of
day. This would be an ideal time to jot down the things they
have meant to you. Some suggestions:

   --List the things that come to mind that you learned from
   them, either through word or example, such as work
   ethic, honesty, integrity, and spirituality, etc.
   --What was the best thing they ever taught you?
   --For a dad, remember to include hunting, fishing,
   golfing, etc.
   --For a mom, include cooking, sewing, art, etc.

--Think about what made them different, did they have funny little sayings that you'll never forget?

For a meaningful gift anytime, consider doing the same thing for grandparents, siblings, spouse, and/or children.

In the event that your parents have already passed, somehow they already know how much they meant to you. Write down your memories of them anyway, perhaps in an open letter to them, so that your descendants and other family members will know how special they were.

Setting Goals for a New Year

No matter what your age, if you don't have a "bucket list", (you know, the things you want to do before you kick the bucket), now is the time to start your personal list. It may be important to put your genealogy research near the top of that list. Now "is" the time, especially if it is something you always wanted to do, while there are people and resources that can still answer your questions.

As one year draws to a close and a new one begins, we are reminded to take stock of the year we left behind. It is exciting to plan for what we expect the New Year to hold. Usually, the best starting point is examining what we had planned to do in the past year and where we fell short of it. Some may call them resolutions, but I prefer to call them goals. Were they written down? Were the goals realistic to begin with? Were they manageable? Most of all, did you create a plan to get there? If your answer is no to any of these questions, chances are good that you were not able to make it a reality. The best of intentions will not make it viable unless we make a plan.

However, there is no good to be gained from beating ourselves up over perceived failures. Think of it as just a delayed plan and vow to make the New Year the best it can be. We are in charge. Will this be the year we make major changes in our lives? Will it be the year we finally accomplish one or more of our goals? Even if we don't get there by the end of the coming year, it will still be a goal to work on in the next. Be sure to put any unfinished business near the top of your list for the New Year.

There have no doubt been many joys, sorrows, and perhaps some disappointments. These sorrows are a normal part of life. It is what we learn from them, and how we use the experience, that make a difference in our lives, just as it did in the lives of our ancestors

To achieve balance in our lives, the plan should include multiple areas. The first thing to do is to make a list of goals for each area of our life. Remember to set goals high enough so that you have something to reach for, but again, keep in mind they must be realistic in order to be achievable. Goal planning should be written down.

Suggestion: write these categories on a sheet of notebook paper in a vertical column.

--Health
--Spirituality
--Family
--Career
--Financial

--Relationships
--Education…and don't forget to include
--Fun and leisure…this includes making time for
yourself and doing some of those things that you really
want to do for your emotional health.

Then at the top, create a horizontal column of timelines,
with at least three headings or more. Be specific as to what
you want and by when you want to accomplish it. If we
don't have a goal in mind, we probably aren't going to get
there any time soon. They would be:

--Short term--meaning soon
--Intermediate--say within six months
--Long term--eventually, but with a time frame in mind.

Now, fill it in and be honest with yourself. For each
area, under the timelines, list the steps that will make them
manageable. Some may be revealed as you go along, and
that's okay. Make a list of possible setbacks and possible
remedies. Now you have a plan. Include notes as you go
along and be flexible. Review and revise your list at least
every couple of weeks, making necessary adjustments.

It is extremely satisfying to see your progress become a
reality both in person and on paper. The only person who can
change our reality is "ourselves". Taking personal
responsibility is one of the most challenging but rewarding
things we can ever do.

Unless you are a person who has time on their hands to
fill, obviously you are not able to make use of all the ideas

and suggestions that have been presented throughout these pages. However, I hope you have been able to make use of as many of them as you could fit into your lifestyle to make your research a little easier and a lot more fun. It is always later than we think.

The Changing Times

Somewhere between the ages of 40 and 50, we begin to realize, like it or not, that life is all about change. For some of us, it happens earlier than for others. But whatever the case may be, the one sure thing that we can count on is that nothing in life (as we know it) can ever stay the same. If it did, we would have no occasion to grow and learn. Most of us think of it as a sad thing, especially when loss is involved, and particularly at holiday time. Our ancestors absolutely, went through the same feelings we have and surely made decisions based on those experiences. As we research, we may find out things that occurred that resulted from those choices. Remember to keep an open mind and not be judgmental of those who have gone before us. Like us, they probably based their decisions on their emotions at the time.

Every aspect of our lives has certainly changed from that of our forefathers. Everything from technology to morality has changed, and so it will too, for the next generations to come. The old adage of what is old shall become new again has often occurred and become part of the circle of life.

As you research, you will possibly find that one or more of your ancestors probably suffered from some form of depression at one time or another in their lives, just as they did physical ailments. Of course, these again impacted the choices they made in their lives.

Change is not an easy concept to deal with because it means we might have to leave our comfort zone. However, life's very purpose is to change and grow. Some of us steadfastly refuse to accept change, not realizing that we are limiting ourselves. We are all guilty at times of not living life the way it was intended. Maybe because it reminds us we are getting older, or have regrets, or simply don't want to.

However, what if we were to think of "change" as someone opening new doors and new chapters in our life? Our whole perspective would change. We would no longer have a fear of the unknown. Instead we would look forward with eager anticipation to finding out what life has to offer us next. That doesn't mean it would take all pain, trial and tribulation away, but it will definitely make it easier to bear. What if we embrace change instead of refusing and avoiding it? It's kind of like having a "Plan B". Yes, it requires acceptance of it and that may not be an easy thing to do. However, once we do accept it, we can look forward to many new experiences. It will make a phenomenal difference in our lives, and can also be one of the best remedies for depression that there is (not that anyone should give up their currently prescribed medications).

*****

A final thought--thus far, this book has largely been based on the importance of finding and preserving our heritage for those who come after us. While it is important for us to know our roots, it is even more important to understand how we are affected now in the greater scheme of things and how our actions will affect our own descendants.

When the values and beliefs that have been handed down through generations no longer serve us in our current world, maybe it is time to take a closer look at them. This will take courage because it may mean changing some or all of the core values of our ancestors. As much as we loved and cherished them, it doesn't mean their attitudes and values are or were right for us. They were, like all of us, just doing the best they could with the information they had at the time.

Depending on the situation, perhaps it is not even something we should strive to instill in our own children or grandchildren. Because times have changed, what worked for our ancestors may now no longer work for us personally or as a species. After all, we will someday be the ancestors of future generations. How do we want them to look back on us?

It is time for humanity to reassess what is truly in our best highest purpose. This will require change for all of us on the inside before it can be expressed outwardly. Furthermore, it is becoming increasingly evident that the future of our planet depends on it.

For further information on what you can do to play your part, please see Book 1 of "Conversations With Humanity", by Neale Donald Walsch. Yes, you CAN make a difference.

*****

If you have enjoyed searching for your roots and have uncovered some fascinating details on the lives of your ancestors, you are invited to consider taking genealogy to an entirely new level with Jami's new book in progress, to be entitled,

"The Genealogy of Past Lives,
Taking it to the Next Level".

In it, you will discover how to learn about, document, and research your past lives over a span of hundreds, if not thousands of years.

In addition, you will realize the lessons you have come to learn and how they pertain to the current life.

For details, visit:

www.jamilynnsands.com
www.blessedbyspirit.com

Many blessings,

Jami Lynn

*****

Glossary

(As related to the subject of genealogy)

Ancestor—a person/relative from whom one has descended, meaning having preceded you (that you may or may not have known)

Ancestral village—city, town, village or locality of an ancestor's birth

Ancestry—family descent, or ancestors collectively

Archive—a documentary or a place to keep documented records

Artifacts—any object made by human work

Bloodline—line of direct descent, related by blood

Bookplate—a label placed in or on a book to identify it or it's owner

Consort of—old world term for a spouse

Cover page—The top page used in manuscripts, legacy writing, journals, etc. to identify a document's title and contents

Crypt—an underground burial vault

Descendant—the offspring of, having come from, usually referring to those who follow or come after

Documentation—in genealogy, it refers to the acquiring of documents generally used to validate lineage

Epitaph—a memorial inscription on a tomb

Ethnic—a group of people having common customs, characteristics, language, etc.

Format—the plan, layout, shape, size or arrangement of a book

Genealogy—a recorded history of a person's ancestry, the study of someone's lineage

Generations—the producing of offspring, a single stage in the succession of descent

Heirlooms—any treasured possession handed down from one generation to another

Heritage—property or tradition handed down from the past or ancestors

Kinship—family relationship or close connection

Legacy—money, property or anything handed down from an ancestor

Legacy writing—written account of our own hopes and dreams (or those of our ancestors) for those we will leave behind, often includes our/their beliefs and ideals

Lineage—direct descent from an ancestor

Mausoleum—a tomb or a building with spaces or drawers for entombing multiple bodies

Memorabilia—things serving as a record or a reminder

Memoir—an autobiography, based on the writer's personal knowledge

Memento—a souvenir

Monochromatic—referring to a color scheme, shades or tones of one color, (sometimes used with neutrals for contrast)

Nationality—the status of belonging to a nation by birth or naturalization

Networking—the developing of contacts or exchanging of information

Post mortem photography—meaning "after death", photographs of the deceased

Query—to question, an inquiry

Ship manifests—port of entry documents detailing a ship's log, usually includes ship's cargo and any pertinent information available on passengers and crew

Surname—a last name, the family name

Time capsule—a collection of data, documents or memorabilia pertinent to the past stored for safe keeping and intended to be opened at a certain time in the future, in the case of genealogy, usually for descendants

Timeline—a chronological chart or list of events, dates, plans, etc.

Vellum—a fine but strong parchment paper used for writing and/or memory book making, usually transparent

*****

BIBLIOGRAPHY

General research:

www.ancestordig.com

www.ancestry.com

www.archives.gov

www.books.google.com
(The National Archives and
Records Administration)

census.gov/genealogy/www/agesearch.ml
(US census records)

www.familysearch.org
(Mormon family records)

www.findagrave.com

www.freegenealogytools.com

www.free-peoplesearch.com/deceased

www.genealogy.about.com

www.genealogybank.com

www.GeneaSearch.comwww.newspaperarchive.com
(for a little additional, you will have   access to
_Godfrey Memorial Library)

www.ngsgenealogy.org
(National Genealogy Society)

www.rootsweb.com

www.searchforancestors.com

www.searchgenealogy.net

www.WorldVitalRecords.com

www.worldcat.org
(World library information)

www.USApeoplesearch.com
www.usgenweb.org

Port of entry & ship_manifest records:

www.EllisIsland.org

www.genesearch.com/ports.html

Inspirational credit:

www.josephsoninstitute.org
(Josephson Institute 2011/
Poem reprinted with permission).

www.nealedonaldwalsch.com
Neale Donald Walsch, author,
"Conversations with God"
"Conversations with Humanity"

Miscellaneous:

createspace.com

Google Earth

Mapquest.com

youtube.com

In addition,

State Libraries usually have a Genealogy Department
(check with state capital)

RESOURCES/CREDITS

Franco, Carol and Kent Lineback, *The Legacy Guide.*
Penguin Group, 2006. (Wonderful for further information
and ideas)

Rodgers and Hammerstein/Carousel

Webster's New World Dictionary

*****

About the author

Jami Lynn Sands

Jami is an Ohio native with a passion for our history. What started out as a scrapbooking project in 2007 with a goal of making heritage albums for her children, turned into an awesome journey to find both the stories and facts of their heritage. She is passionate about the urgency of researching and preserving the past for future generations to know their roots.

Jami enjoys writing on a variety of topics, both fiction and non-fiction, including human-interest stories and life experiences. She is also author of a newspaper column on genealogy research tips and ideas that she has contributed to

a local paper for over five years. Over the years, she has also
had many short stories published as a member of several
writing groups. In addition to writing her own material, she
enjoys the challenge of "ghostwriting" and is eager to tell
your story.

Other interests include travel, reading and studying,
scrapbooking, natural healing, and exploring the
metaphysical. She enjoys spending part of the year in
Sedona, Arizona and part on the Virginia--Carolina coast.

Jami Lynn may be contacted
through email at:

jami@jamilynnsands.com

jamilynnsands@yahoo.com

Website:
www.jamilynnsands.com

*****

NOTES

NOTES

NOTES

NOTES

NOTES